LESSONS FROM THE VOYAGE OF LIFE

ACTS 27:6–44

Robert Cox

Published by

MELROSE BOOKS

An Imprint of Melrose Press Limited
St Thomas Place, Ely
Cambridgeshire
CB7 4GG, UK
www.melrosebooks.co.uk

FIRST EDITION

Copyright © Robert Cox 2012

The Author asserts his moral right to
be identified as the author of this work

Cover designed by Scott Gwinnett

ISBN 978-1-908645-06-7

Printed and bound in Great Britain by:
CPI Antony Rowe, Chippenham, Wiltshire

TABLE OF CONTENTS

I wish to express my gratitude to the following people
who helped me in the writing of this book.

To Ronald Evans of the Rhondda Valley
to whom I owe an enormous debt for his dedication
in typing up the original manuscript.

To Trudi Priscilla Phelps
for painstakingly dealing with the corrections
that needed to be made during the editing process.

To Joanna Bowden
who kindly painted the cover picture
which so aptly depicts the theme of this book.

INTRODUCTION

The Acts of the Apostles is a narrative of the history of the Church in its very early, formative beginnings, whose story is that of indispensable preparation for eternity, through the good offices of the LORD Jesus Christ and the Gospel of full salvation made available by His sufferings and atoning death, followed by His resurrection. Paul's last voyage en route to Rome, filled with high drama and crisis, is a fitting epilogue to the general tenor of the narrative. Every verse virtually is rich in truth and adds its imagery to the elaborate tapestry of the Acts of the Apostles.

SERMON 1

A SHIP OF ALEXANDRIA

Acts 27:6: *And there the centurion found a ship of Alexandria sailing into Italy; and he put us therein.*

The first leg of Paul's journey, along with certain other prisoners, was completed when the ship of Adramyttium nosed its way into Myra, a city of Lycia. At Myra an Alexandrian grain ship was about to cast anchor which was routed for Italy, into which Julian the centurion shepherded the prisoners and their escorting Roman soldiers. 'Myra', meaning 'I flow', or 'I pour out', or 'I weep' could well have been a divine presagement of a disastrous voyage, fulfilling the dictum, "coming events cast their shadows beforehand". Perhaps Paul's chains and Roman guards were brought home to him, as he must have reflected of his free condition en route to Jerusalem and his changed circumstances outward bound for Rome. Had he taken God's message, given so dramatically by Agabus more than two years earlier, he would still have been God's ambassador at large with the Gospel, so familiarized with him that he called it, 'his Gospel', and always accompanied with a power second to none.

Of the seven travellers at that time with him, Aristarchus and Luke alone made up his company. Luke was earmarked to be the Church's future historian. Had he been absent, the events of the forthcoming melodrama would never have been known. Aristarchus was one of his fellow travellers, who had stuck with him, even sharing his prison incarceration and manhandling by the mob in Ephesus, along with Gaius, where Aristarchus barely escaped with his life when bundled into the theatre. Little known

1

to him, he would experience another hairsbreadth escape on the forthcoming voyage. Apostles live dangerously, and they who are companions of the LORD's pioneers share the same danger. Like James and John, called to drink of the same cup that Christ their LORD and Master drank of, Paul's aides had no reason to expect less.

Julius, the centurion of Augustus' band, had been put in charge of Paul and his fellow prisoners. Their cases were to be heard before Nero and almost certainly involved issues of life and death. Julius was undoubtedly a centurion of note for his cohorts were of the Italian band with reason to believe they formed part of the Praetorian Guard.

Paul's relationship with Julius was an amicable one. Already Julius had courteously allowed Paul leave of absence to visit his friends at Sidon. It is not at all improbable that Julius had been present with the chief captains at the last hearing of the apostle before Festus and King Agrippa, and came from that private hearing greatly impressed with the bearing and testimony of the most extraordinary man he had ever met, Festus and Nero included, not least the calmness and manliness with which Paul answered Festus. The good offices of the Roman centurion would, under God, save Paul's life from the viciousness of the Roman soldiers before the end of the voyage.

Amongst the cordage at the Port of Myra the centurion found a grain ship of Alexandria, which was bound for Italy. Its tonnage and draught was ideal for the large company waiting to be tran-shipped – composed of a not inconsiderable number of Roman legionaries and presumably more than a sprinkling of political prisoners with passengers such as Luke and Aristarchus. With the unknown number making up the crew, they comprised a grand company of 276 personnel. Unless the ship had been unusually spacious, the deck or the well of the ship would have been greatly congested, and a large grain cargo would have dangerously increased her ballast.

In that era there was no Plimsoll line, and greedy merchants often loaded their ships to the gunwale, and endangered the lives of the crew. Heavy seas easily swept over the sides and sank the ships.

Egypt had been the granary of a large section of the Roman world. Wheat had been one of its chief products. The alluvial soil of the Nile, deposited yearly from the flooding by the headwaters, yielded prolific harvests. Pharaoh's dreams of the soil bringing forth by handfuls readily confirm the claim of repeated bumper crops.

Paul would have been reminded of grain of another kind for which the city was world famous. It boasted one of the largest libraries in the world, but the most famous of all its books was the Septuagint translation of the Hebrew Scriptures, and deriving its name from the seventy Greek scholars who translated the Scriptures into the Greek language. Ever since, it has vied with all other Hebrew translations.

The apostle to the Gentiles was no stranger to travelling by sea, being as used to it as the modern traveller is habituated to travelling by air. Numbers of times had he been in peril while journeying by sea. He relates that on three occasions he had been shipwrecked, one of which left him twenty-four hours in the deep, probably holding onto a spar or some flotsam and jetsam left floating after the ship on which he had been sailing had sunk and plunged him into the water. We would like to have known who picked him up and where, but such details, characteristically, are passed over in silence in a book that has to do with weightier matters and the salvation of the souls of men.

The ensuing narrative is the record of the vagaries of a voyage that simulate the experiences of humans en route from this world to the next, but more especially those of Christian persuasion with their various trials, and their ultimate hope of heaven. It has been well called *The Voyage of Life*, and its relation is replete with incidents and verses that pinpoint a medley of spiritual truths.

Paul at the outset could not have suspected the nature of the ordeal that would be his and his fellow travellers' lot on that stretch of water between Myra and Melita. Of one thing only was he sure: that as he had borne powerful witness to the LORD at Jerusalem, so he would glorify God at Rome, in bearing witness to Him before Nero, the most ferocious of the Cæsars (Acts 23:11), and before the voyage was completed he would have witnessed a good confession to every member of the ship's crew and company, and have netted more fish than Peter and the disciples' 153 great fishes when Christ revealed Himself to the disciples for the third time after His resurrection (John 21:14).

* * * * * * * * * * * * * * * * * * * *

SERMON 2

THE FAIR HAVENS

Acts 27:7–*8: And when we had sailed slowly many days, and scarce were come over against Cnidus, the wind not suffering us, we sailed under Crete, over against Salmone; And, hardly passing it, came unto a place which is called The Fair Havens; nigh whereunto was the city of Lasea.*

INTRODUCTION:

The beginning of the voyage did not augur well for the success of the journey. Paul and his fellow travellers were dogged by a stiff breeze – called a contrary wind – from the west. With great difficulty and skilful seamanship the vessel was nosed inside the harbour or possibly the breakwater, and not for nothing called 'the Fair Havens'. Usually havens are places of refuge, especially in connection with storms at sea. Perhaps the port of the text is expressly called "fair" because of the protection it afforded against a foul and blustering sea.

God is said to control the winds, for it is written, "He holds the winds in His fist", and if, as is stated, that a straw will indicate the direction of the wind, betimes the wind itself can betoken the direction of God's will. When Columbus in his voyage to find an eastern route to the Indies was tacking a north-westerly course contrary to the prevailing wind, his crew members said, "Master, follow the wind", and in doing so discovered the West Indies. He missed North America, for God had other plans than that of its being colonized by Roman Catholic Spain. That same God directed His winds to drive the Spanish Armada onto the rocky coast of the north-west of Britain, thus wrecking it, for the same

5

reason as He would not have them take possession of the vast and wealthy continent of North America.

Here, however, the opposing wind could well have been an attempt by the prince of the powers of the air to prevent the apostle turning up at Rome, and later the pressure was stepped up even more. Satan knew that God had made an appointment for Paul to confront Nero and his court which was the vilest on the face of the globe. Of all people in this world Satan feared Paul the most. Paul's ambition, as was more than hinted at in 2 Tim.4:17 was that he should preach to the Emperor as it says, "that by me the preaching might be fully known, and that all the Gentiles might hear: and I was delivered out of the mouth of the lion" meaning deliverance at the confrontation with Caesar.

Earlier in the Acts of the Apostles, they, when called to go over to Macedonia, in a vision by night, proceeded to "Samothracia by a straight course and the following day were at Neapolis and from there to the chief city of that part of Macedonia called Philippi" (Acts 16:9–12). All the lights were green, with no contrary winds.

Adjacent to the Fair Havens was the city of Lasea, which means thick or wise. From the traumatic events that followed their hasty departure out of the Fair Havens it is patent that God had intended them to winter there. It was a kind of half-way house between them and their destination, thus it is with the only haven that offers rest to those mariners and voyagers storm-tossed on the troubled sea of a guilty conscience. There is no retreat fairer or more secure than the Gospel, and no more meaningful question has ever been asked than "How shall we escape if we neglect so great salvation" (Heb.2:3). "For neither is there salvation in any other: for there is none other name under heaven given among men, whereby we must be saved" (Acts 4:12).

Perhaps because of the nearness of the City of Lasea, which means wisdom, you would argue the wisdom of using the harbour of the Fair Havens for the duration of the inclement weather conditions typical of the period of winter. An old adage has it:

"Any port in a storm" but the Gospel of Jesus Christ, sometimes termed 'the Gospel of Peace', loudly calls, "the *only* port in a storm". King Jehoshaphat's merchant fleet, built at Ezion Geber to trade in gold at Tarshish, was broken up even before breaking the waters outside the port. An unholy alliance with Ahaziah son of Ahab stymied the project: God had handed the fleet over to the elements, which are the respecters of none.

Christ's invitation holds good without qualification: "Come unto Me all ye that labour and are heavy laden" ... "anxious concerning your sins and your souls' salvation" (John Wesley) "and I will give you rest. Take My yoke upon you and learn of Me; for I am meek and lowly in heart: and ye shall find rest unto your souls. For My yoke is easy, and My burden is light" (Matt.11: 28–9).

As long as faith is conjoined with a good conscience, the refugee is as secure in Christ the Fair Haven as in heaven itself. There is no possibility of shipwreck. Before any such catastrophe "the good conscience has to be put away – literally thrust away – for it never goes willingly". (John Wesley). Unfortunately, as Paul observed, some have foolishly parted with their good conscience and made shipwreck of their faith, and a wrecked ship is never salvaged: "Holding faith, and a good conscience; which some having put away concerning faith have made shipwreck" (1 Tim.1:19). Hymenaeus and Alexander were two such, and were delivered to Satan, that they might learn not to blaspheme (verse 20).

One major criticism of the Fair Haven was its incommodious location. Not a few fault-finders complained it was not spacious enough and needed more latitude to allow for elbow room. They pointed out the haven was not commodious to spend the winter there (verse 12). Complaints of this nature against Christ and the Gospel have been a feature from the outset. People cry out that Christianity is too narrow; it needs to broaden its outlook, and in so doing will attract more people to its cause. All of this countermands the clear presentation of Christ to the contrary, whose words were, "Enter ye in at the strait gate: for wide is the gate, and broad is the way that leadeth to destruction, and many there be that go in thereat: because strait is the gate, and narrow is the way which leadeth unto life, and few there be that find it" (Matt.7:13–14). This the LORD demonstrated in the case of the wealthy young ruler who humbly appealed to Christ for admission into the Kingdom of Heaven, but who returned home because Christ's terms of entry demanded the disposing of his vast wealth, which drew from Christ the much-quoted saying: "It is easier for a camel to go through the eye of a needle than for a rich man to enter the Kingdom of God" (Matt.19:16–26). It has been suggested that the needle was the small wicket gate, let into the main gates, and for a camel to enter through that gate required a lot of manoeuvring and that its load be removed from its back. In the Bible the camel is often used as a type of a rich man.

In the parable of the great supper, in which all the invited guests initially gave notice of acceptance but rudely declined on the eve of the feast, offering very lame excuses, an angry lord gave an immediate order to go into the city's streets and lanes and bring in the poor, the blind, the lame and the maimed which having been carried out and in spite of this order being carried out there was still room for more, there was yet space for more (Luke 14:16–22). The story equates to the great supper of the Gospel. For 2000 years the invitations have been given and received by the millions of sinners of every description, when offered by the LORD's ministers and servants, only to hear the announcement is still, "Yet there is room!" Eventually, the final census will reveal a company whom no man can number, with room and enough to spare (Rev.7:9). There may be no room for Christ in man's inn – his heart – yet in God's abode there are many mansions, each one reserved for those "who have been begotten again unto a living hope, by the resurrection of Jesus Christ from the dead" (1 Peter 1:3).

A winter's quarters at the Fair Havens demanded discipline; there was no room for laxity. Christian character makes self-discipline a prerequisite, and referred to by Christ as "taking up one's cross", the absence of which precludes true discipleship. To a mixed company of the people with His disciples, whom He had called together, He proclaimed, "Whosoever will come after Me, let him deny himself, and take up his cross and follow Me" (Mark 8:34).

To be in Christ is to become Christ-like, who figuratively has been described as "the chiefest of ten thousands. He is altogether lovely" (Song of Sol.5:10, 16). Small wonder that the glowing tribute He pays His spouse is that she is "fair as the moon" (Song of Sol.6:10). Like the moon, her fairness is reflected from the Sun of Righteousness (Song of Sol.1:16). Only when the moon is full and rounded is it defined as fair, and so the Loved One of the Canticle, when she is full with the blessing of the LORD, and of the Holy Ghost, and rounded in the likeness of His perfection does she truly reflect His beauty of holiness. Those who are shy of the Fair Havens are lacking in character and moral fibre.

* * * * * * * * * * * * * * * * * * * *

SERMON 3

PAUL'S SEASONABLE WARNING

Acts 27:9: *Now when much time was spent, and when sailing was now dangerous, because the fast was now already past, Paul admonished them, and said unto them, "Sirs, I perceive that this voyage will be with hurt and much damage, not only of the lading and ship, but also of our lives".*

INTRODUCTION:

Like Ezekiel, called God's Watchman, who had received express instructions to warn the House of Israel (Ezek.3:17) so Paul had received word from Heaven to alert the captain-owner of the ship and Julian the commanding officer of the military presence and of the prisoners, of certain disaster if they left their present refuge for Phenice – some twenty leagues further along the coast of Crete.

The apostle's warning was specific, both as to the gravity of the disaster and the source of his intelligence, which was more than intuition. His spiritual faculties had received a revelation from God by which he perceived the unfolding drama of the loss of the ship and the valuable cargo, with their lives at great risk. Like a faithful watchman he delivered the warning, though probably at the time of his warning the day was serene, the sky without a cloud, and the sea as calm as a millpond. Most people's prognostications are little more than constructions placed on present events of a foreboding nature. Men who know their God speak unequivocally when the tenor of their message is contradicted by the prevailing conditions. When George Fox the pioneer of the Quaker movement, called 'the Society of Friends', predicted the fall of the Long Parliament, which was sitting under Cromwell's

Commonwealth, he did so when this parliament seemed set for a further extended period. His prediction was given in the presence of eminent judges and justices, and included the actual day it would be dissolved. Briefly, he said, "This day week the Long Parliament will fall." The precise day was a Wednesday, and as the servant of the LORD foretold, the Long Parliament was disbanded.

Paul's warning was delivered under divine inspiration, which coincided with the features of immediate concern, and were prefaced by the word "now".

Firstly the word "now" stressed that already much time had been spent. In short, valuable time had been lost on arrival at their present sanctuary. Any additional delay in trying to negotiate a further stretch of water could be fatal. The current delay had reduced the time schedule to a minimum. Time was the most precious commodity that these travellers possessed apart from their souls, and for the Christian its value is only inferior to their salvation. Paul exhorted some of the Ephesian believers to awake from the sleep of "sloth and spiritual death and stupid insensibility" (John Wesley) and to make amends by "redeeming the time, because of the godless age and evil days they were living in" (Ephes.5:14, 16).

To redeem is to buy back, and no doubt enshrines the idea of buying back all possible time from sin and Satan, even retrieving it from ease and sloth and pleasure, to say nothing of business and other lawful as well as laudable pursuits. Reinvest it in the best purposes and spiritual exercises, performing works for the good of being and the salvation of the souls of men. In the modern age the bulk of people's leisure time is swallowed up by television, the telephone and multiple holidays.

Time has been given to prepare for eternity, and neither a day more than is necessary. Lord Chesterfield, the man of letters, whose company was courted more than any other man of his day by aristocracy and men of eminence, expressed his dismay in the closing period of his life at his wasted years and the vanity of his pursuits. He likened his endeavours to those of chasing butterflies and grasping at cobwebs and gathering dust. So taken up with the plot and gaudy scenery of the play had he been, that he had not bothered to go backstage and see the dusty machinery of the pulleys and ropes and ugly impedimenta that propped up the glittering scene. Voltaire, taken suddenly ill, enquired anxiously of his physician how much time he could assure him of, to be told "none", and ejaculated, "Then I shall go to hell, and you will go with me!" A bishop once wrote a treatise on the soul and concluded his sermon with telling words: "I have but one soul and I will value it" and such is only truly evaluated when all possible time is expended on its spiritual culture. John Ruskin, an able writer and philosopher, said, "I wake up every morning with twenty-four golden sovereigns in my purse, each one studded with sixty diamond minutes. I will value them."

Secondly, the word "now" emphasised that "sailing was dangerous". Sailing, understandably, is never without its dangers, not even in the calmest of waters. One of its hazards is its fickle-ness, when sudden squalls can turn it into a raging cauldron. One of its hazards is the fickleness of the elements when sudden squalls can turn the waters into a raging cauldron. This is much like the tenor of life when seemingly there is little danger to disturb its equanimity and then as the saying runs out of a blue, cloud-free sky a bolt comes to precipitate disaster. We see this in the case of Job when the report was brought to him that the fire of God had fallen from Heaven – that is the lightning – and that it had burned up the sheep and his servants and consumed them (Job 1:16).

Spiritual danger for the believer is never far away, which is the reason he is exhorted to "be sober, be vigilant; because your adversary the devil, as a roaring lion, walketh about, seeking whom he may devour" (1 Peter 5:8). Satan never runs, but walks, that he might the more easily see and devour unwary sleepers. In his catalogue of perils listed among his many sufferings, Paul adverts to eight different kinds he was constantly exposed to, yet were they the norm of the apostle to the Gentiles. Never are we without the need to pray, "Lead us not into temptation, but deliver us from evil" (Matt.6:13). False brethren were classified among Paul's perils in reference to which Jude revealed in his short epistle that there were certain men crept in unawares, literally as by a side door, whom Christ called "sheep-stealers", "who enter the fold other than by the door" (John 10:1). Those referred to by Jude he called "ungodly men turning the grace of our God into lasciviousness" (Jude 4). Later in his epistle Jude further enlarged upon their character, calling them "spots in your Feasts of Charity" (verse 12). Literally the meaning is that they were sunken or hidden rocks, and many a gallant ship has split its beam on an uncharted rock, whereas the Rock of Gibraltar is so conspicuous that the smallest ship can avoid it.

Psalm 107 tells of four classes of men from the four cardinal points of the compass, whom the LORD had redeemed from the hand of the enemy, and delivered from the incidence of what was certain death, and were spared in the nick of time by their crying unto God in their trouble, and bringing them out of their distresses (Psalm 107:6, 13 ,19, 28). Of the four citations, the last treating of the danger and distresses of "those who go down to the sea in ships and do business in great waters; these see the works of the LORD and His wonders in the deep". Psalm 107:23–4 gives the most graphic and gripping description of the sailors' predicament of whom it is recorded that "they are at their wits' end" (verse 27). Like the others in their distresses they cry unto the LORD in their trouble, and He bringeth them out of their distresses (verse 28). In the era of sails and the tall ships there was a saying current among sailors: "If a man would learn to pray, let him go to sea."

As mentioned above the word "now" secondly highlighted the type of impending danger that is out of the normal run of hazards. The type that needs an immediate decision which here was needed to preserve their lives from the tragedy of being sunk at sea without trace. When God gives direct warning of impending disaster, it is the veriest madness to ignore it. A concealed rock was once suspected of wrecking vessels in the Mediterranean, and was eventually marked on the navigational chart. The skipper of a large passenger boat discredited the claimed location, and said he would prove incontrovertibly that the claim was spurious. As his ship drew near the supposed latitude and longitude where it was newly charted, he boasted as he sailed his boat right over the mark that then would be the moment of truth, and it was: the rock ripped the bottom apart, so that within a short while the boat sank. As far as memory serves me, the captain could not face the music and committed suicide. His action was criminal negligence.

Something of the same nature involved the grain ship of Alexandria in a parallel saga. The ship was set to avoid all the warning lights and a red flag hung from the battlements of Heaven. God has given the world, especially the Church, a chart and compass called the Bible. Every sunken rock of spurious religion is charted; dangerous currents of temptation and lust are clearly marked; the prevailing winds of false doctrines are as patently noted as the trade winds on a royal ordinance geographical map of the world. Joshua was a God-fearing man, but he was out of bounds when he sallied forth from Jerusalem to intercept Pharaoh Necho who had a large army which was en route to engage the Babylonians and prevent them taking over the denuded and fast breaking up Assyrian Empire. Even Necho had a message from God for Josiah and told him not to meddle. With the bit between his teeth, however, Josiah carried on even though the Word of God pointed against him. Josiah met his Waterloo when much like King Ahab, who disguised himself, the arrows of the archers found the chinks in his armour. His chariot, therefore, was no triumphal car back to his capital, but an anticipation of the hearse that would carry him to his sepulchre. Ominously, his citation reads "He hearkened not to the words of Necho from the mouth of God". No one ever escaped scot free who deliberately ignored the red flag from God. Perhaps he wanted to ingratiate himself with the Babylonians as his grandfather Hezekiah had done only to receive notice from Isaiah of his folly with a sentence of doom for his heirs.

The urgency of the third "Now" is drawn from the passing of the fast, which sounds as if that important date was the deadline for sailing that stretch of sea. It coincided with the Autumnal equinox but applies to the Jewish Day of Atonement, which was one of national mourning for and confession of the Jewish people's sins. On that most important of all days in the sacred calendar of the Jews, a goat was offered in the Tabernacle for the nation's sins. Another goat had all the sins of the people recited over and imparted to it, before being led away and left in a place where no man lived. Pictorially and typically, their sins were atoned for and cancelled, and the people were at liberty to carry on their normal lives for another year. All the ceremonies were fulfilled by Christ, who bore the sins of the whole world in His body on the cross and secured liberty once and for all time and eternity for all who heartily believe. Paul most certainly alluded to this in his second letter to the Corinthians, and quotes Isaiah as his authority: "For He saith I have heard thee in a time accepted, and in the Day of Salvation have I succoured thee: behold now is the accepted time; behold now is the Day of Salvation" (Isaiah 49:8). John the Baptist drew attention to it when he pinpointed Christ, who came to him the day after His baptism, and pointing Him out said, "Behold the Lamb of God who taketh away [literally "beareth away"] the sin of the world" (John 1:29) not of that nation only, as on the Day of Atonement, but universally so. God's timetable for potential beneficiaries is now; His Day of Salvation to today. The question posed in Hebrews is "How shall we escape if we neglect so great salvation?" Heb.2:3 has peculiar relevance to this event. To be casual or indifferent to it is rashly to invite the certain disaster implicit in the warning. When that Fast or Atonement is bypassed "there remains no further sacrifice for sins, but a certain fearful looking for of judgement and fiery indignation ... he that despised Moses' Law died without mercy under two or three witnesses: of how much sorer punishment, suppose ye, shall he be thought worthy, who hath trodden underfoot the Son of God, and hath counted the blood of the covenant wherewith he hath been sanctified an unholy thing ... For we know Him that hath said, 'Vengeance belongeth unto Me, I will recompense,' saith the LORD" (Heb.10:26–30).

A story is told of a young man rowing his boat down the Niagara River and coming to the notice that said, "This is the point of no return". Foolishly he imagined he could let his boat drift a little further before turning back, only to discover that the warning given was unexceptionable, and he was swept over the Falls by the increasingly swift flowing current.

Isaiah opens his prophecy with a scorching diatribe against Judah and Israel. God's complaint was that the domestic animals – the ox and the ass – had far greater respect for their masters than the people of God for their LORD, and calls the heavens and the earth to hear his invective, saying, "I have nourished and brought up children, and they have rebelled against Me. The ox knoweth his owner, and the ass his master's crib: but Israel doth not know, My people doth not consider. Ah sinful nation, a people laden with iniquity, a seed of evildoers, children that are corrupters, they have forsaken the LORD ... they have gone away backward" (Isaiah 1:2–4). Even so, in spite of such withering criticism God's love blazes through, as it were, "showing Himself through the lattice" (Song of Sol.2:9). The criss-cross work of our sins, far from a complete dissociation, reveals the depth and reality of Christ's love. And rather than break off all association He lovingly appeals for a full reconciliation. Paul astonishingly reveals the intense feelings behind God's love for renewed relationship, declaring, "Now then, we are ambassadors for Christ, as though God did beseech you by us: we pray you in Christ's stead, be ye reconciled to God" (2 Cor.5:20). Wesley said that it is as if God goes on bended knee like a pining suitor seeking the hand of a reluctant bride or a judge appealing to a guilty prisoner to accept pardon. Observe that God's season of reconciliation is "Now". In step with this is a strikingly similar appeal through Isaiah: "Come now, and let us reason together, saith the LORD, though your sins be as scarlet; they shall be as white as snow; though they be red like crimson, they shall be as wool. If ye be willing and obedient, ye shall see the good of the land" (Isaiah 1:18–19).

* *

SERMON 4

AN IRREVOCABLE DECISION

Acts 27:12–15: *Because the haven was not commodious to winter in, the more part advised to depart thence also, if by any means they might attain to Phenice, and there to winter; which is an haven of Crete, and lieth toward the south-west and north-west. And when the south wind blew softly, supposing that they had obtained their purpose, loosing thence, they sailed close by Crete. But not long after there arose against it a tempestuous wind, called Euroclydon.*

Life is the product of decisions. Few things are more essential than the importance of making right ones. Wrong decisions can ruin happiness and lead to disastrous sequels, especially when they cannot be reversed. Millions of people's lives have been ruined because of a marriage partner who was incompatible, and as the marriage union is wrought by God, death alone can dissolve it.

Because of the declared incommodious situation of the Fair Havens it was decided to embark for another port further along the island of Crete and far more inviting, called Phenice, which has overtones in the action of those who remove from the Fair Havens of Gospel peace and security in Christ – of all refuges the safest – not only the safest refuge, but the *only* refuge that spells immunity from the storm of divine judgement in the last day. The Ark of Noah gave him and his family immunity from the judgement of God. That judgement swept over the World and swept away every person outside the Ark. They were still tied up in the delusive charms of this life, eating and drinking, buying and selling, building and planting, marrying and giving in marriage up to the moment when "God opened the windows of Heaven and broke up the fountains of the great deep" (Gen.7:11) This is also much like Demas, one of Paul's companions, of whom the apostle reported, "Demas hath forsaken me, having loved this present world" (2 Tim.4:10). Even Paul's company had become obnoxious.

To the carnal man Christian discipleship soon loses its spiritual appeal and meaning. This can be seen when the appetites of the Israelites in the desert were quickly palled by the divinely provided manna. This manna was described as angel's food, but they lusted after meat and from then onwards became endemic to the diseases of Egypt among which leprosy was paramount. All real Christians, from the commencement of their acceptance in the Beloved Son of God, develop a strong affection for the Bible, and to them it is their rule of faith and conduct, but when it loses its appeal and becomes boring, they opt for something lighter and more entertaining and are soon making plans to embark for the next port.

A preference for Phenice is expressed because it has more to offer "those who mind earthly things, whose god is their belly, whose glory is in their shame" (Phil.3:18–19). They are disenchanted with the austerities of the Christian calling. Their common denominator is the mental menu served up by the television and the media, and of that they never seem to grow weary. Moreover, the geographical location provides a strong clue for the city's popularity: it is said to lie towards the south-west and the north-west, and thereby avoids the extremes of temperature, whether the cold north or the warm south. Its breeze is neither from the torrid south nor the frigid north, but the alternations of both are good, as expressed in the lyric of the Song of Solomon, by the loved maiden: "Awake O north wind, and come thou south; blow upon my garden, that the spices thereof may flow out" (Song of Sol.4:16). Christ's criticism of the Laodicean church was their want of these extremes of experience – that of the cold of tribulation and the heat of revival. John the apostle was "a brother in tribulation in the isle called Patmos for the Word of God and at the same time was in the Spirit on the LORD's Day" (Rev.1:9). The LORD's expressed findings of the Laodiceans' spiritual state were humiliating and He said that those people were "wretched and miserable and poor and blind and naked" (Rev.3:16–17). The bat is classified among the unclean creatures, being neither a mouse nor a bird.

It appears that the captain of the ship was also the owner, and his decision tipped the scales against Paul's warning of the gravity of leaving the Fair Havens before the termination of the winter season. As a seasoned mariner, the captain's reputation for weather lore would be impressive and his opinion would carry much weight. At best, however, he was only a man governed by a limited intellect, of which, the Bible stresses, "receiveth not the things of the Spirit of God". Paul was an intimate of the heavens and the divine controller of the weather, and the architect of the weather pattern, who challenged Job to a contest in respect of the bands of Orion and the sweet influences of the Pleiades: "Canst thou bind the sweet influences of the Pleiades, or loose the bands of Orion?"(Job 38:31). Pleiades is a constellation of stars in the ascendant during the spring, and Orion is in the ascendant during the winter. When God chooses, He turns summer into winter and sends snow at harvest time. A man taught by the Spirit is the peer of the man, however clever, who is directed by human acumen. Joseph and Daniel were better informed than the most erudite in the courts of Pharaoh and Nebuchadnezzar. Joseph was promoted to teach even Pharaoh's senators wisdom. Nevertheless, the full complement of people on board the grain ship from Egypt was primed to believe the captain and owner of the ship rather than the foreboding message of Paul the servant of God. In so doing it was running true to form, for the world will always believe its scientists before God's prophets.

The majority vote secured the verdict, for it appears a

perplexed centurion, with whom rested the final word, took the matter to the ballot box, as it were. As sweeping an assertion as this sounds, the majority are always wrong. Christ intimated as much when speaking of the broad and narrow way, the ways to destruction and heaven respectively. The broad way is frequented by many, but the narrow way by few. Twelve scouts were sent out to bring back their reports on Canaan, which was to be the Israelites' permanent national abode. When put to the vote upon their return as to the advisability of going into Canaan to take immediate possession, two were for and ten were against it, plus 600,000 men of war. Democracy, which bespeaks the rule of the people and hence of the majority, is the weakest form of government. Nebuchadnezzar's composite metal image had more than a heel of Achilles, "...it had feet comprising a mixture of iron and clay, which were shattered into fragments when the uncut stone from heaven fell upon them, and were scattered to the four winds" (Dan.2:31–5).

Julian the centurion was torn between admiration for Paul and the expertise of the ship's captain. But because he was wholly ignorant of God, he devalued the revelation given by Paul. It will always be true that "the natural man receiveth not the things of the Spirit of God, for they are foolishness unto him, neither can he know them for they are spiritually discerned" (1 Cor.2:14). Simple faith has often confounded the wiseacres of this world, even as the little maid of the household of Naaman the Syrian confounded Jehoram the king of Israel (2 Kings 5:3, 6–7).

Ultimately, the wind cast the dice. That was the final deciding factor. "And when the south wind blew softly, supposing they had obtained their purpose, loosing thence, they sailed close by Crete" (Acts 27:13). It would seem the elements were on their side; they could not have wished for a more favourable breeze than that southern zephyr, which was the very antithesis of a blustering north-wester.

There is nothing more fickle than the wind, although a close rival to it is public opinion, which is best ignored with its lamentable reputation. But the wind can blow hot and cold by turns, and the unfolding drama is the direct result of that vagary. It can never be too much insisted upon that providential guidance is insufficient of itself. Jonah the unwilling prophet booked a passage at Joppa in a ship that was about to weigh anchor for Tarshish, his desired destination, but it landed him in the whale's belly, adjacent to hell. All circumstantial guidance needs to be corroborated by a Word from God. Sometimes such guidance is a trick of the devil, and smacks of a kind of decoy leading to an ambush, which is the technique that Satan adopts in seducing the saints, of which the interposition of the south wind in this story is a perfect illustration.

James reminds his readers that none are to say when they are tempted, that they are tempted of God. Rather, "every man is tempted, when he is drawn away of his own lust or desire, and enticed. Then when lust hath conceived it bringeth forth sin: and sin, when it is finished, bringeth forth death" (James 1:13–15). In fine, the desire is conceived within the heart and then appealed to from without or enticed from their safe refuge in Christ by the temptation. When the lust reaches out to the object, sin is conceived, and when sin is consummated, death follows. In this epic story the majority plus the captain and the centurion were strongly in favour of quitting their present sheltered cove or haven – as long as they stayed there, no freak storm or hurricane blast could remove them – but the stirring of the softly blowing south wind was the deciding factor, and immediately they made for the open sea. From then on they were taken over and driven on a crash course.

Their gentle zephyr became a tempest, from which there was no escape. The millpond was transformed into a foaming sea and they were outside the narrows and beyond the harbour bar, with their return to the Fair Havens out of the question. Truly they had cast the die. Their destiny had been, with one fell swoop, taken out of their hands. Not only were they cut off, but left without an escape hatch.

From this story alone, the importance of right decisions cannot be overrated. Eve's wrong decision could not be undone; she had cashiered all her posterity. Eden was bolted and barred. Angels, with all eyes, stood guard, to prevent any attempt by two disgraced humans to plunder the Tree of Life of its fruit of immortality.

Of all the wrong decisions ever made, that of Judas must rank as the most perfidious and costly. He had "betrayed the innocent blood". To undo the deed was his one desire, and with the blood money clutched tightly in his hand, he hastened to the priests, who were not moved by the agony of his conscience, and when heartlessly told by them that there was no more wheeling and dealing; there was no further deal; there would be no undoing, he threw the money down in an agony of frustration. His decision was irreversible.

* * * * * * * * * * * * * * * * * * * *

SERMON 5

CAUGHT – TRICKED BY THE DECEIVER

Acts 27:14–17: *But not long after there arose against it a tempestuous wind, called Euroclydon. And when the ship was caught, and could not bear into the wind, we let her drive ... we had much work to come by the boat.*

Satan's aim is always one of destruction. Christ likened him to a thief, whose stock in trade is "to steal, to kill and to destroy" (John 10:10). From that bent he has never veered since the days of Eden, so that at the end of the Bible he is twice called "that old serpent" (Rev.12:9, 20:2), whose slimy trail can be traced all the way from Eden to this present time, and will continue so until his sequestration, first into the Abyss and finally, a thousand years later, into the lake of fire to join his dupes the Beast and the False Prophet. His activities go back to the cradle of the human race, where he inoculated the innocents Adam and Eve in the Garden of Eden, by which the virus injected conceived the malaise God had warned them of, which would be sin, which in turn would generate death: "As by one man sin entered into the world, and death by sin; and so death passed upon all men, for that all have sinned" (Rom.5:12). God's warning ran, "Dying thou shalt die: death for the body would be gradual, but instantaneously for the spirit" (Gen.2:17).

God's proprietors and wardens of Eden had been caught by trickery or guile. A pleasurable bait snatched at produced a disastrous end. Icelanders used herrings to catch cod. Satan is canny enough to know that to confront men as the Prince of Darkness would terrify them. Consequently, he appears as the Angel of Light, and as such his seductions are hard, but not impossible to resist. Absalom's charm and kiss of affection, accompanied by his fair promises, "stole away the hearts of the men of Israel" (2 Sam.15:6).

Satan's ace card was well concealed – out of sight in the east – in the hemisphere known to Bible students as the place of estrangement from God. Cain, in high dudgeon, "left the presence of God and dwelt in the land of Nod", meaning 'wandering', "east of Eden" (Gen.4:16). No sooner were Paul and his fellow travellers lured out of the narrows onto the high seas, than Euroclydon took over. It was labelled a tempestuous wind, which is a compound word made up of 'the east wind and the wave'.

Satan has been called "the prince of the powers of the air" – a theatre of malign spirits, which is the same spirit that "now worketh in the children of disobedience" (Ephes.2:2). God, whose power is over all, and who holds the winds in His fist, sometimes in the outworking of His secret purposes allows the evil one to harness the elements to carry out his wicked designs, as when Christ was asleep in the boat on the lake of Galilee and with His disciples was crossing to the other side. Taking advantage of a recumbent and sleeping Christ, Satan stirred up a great storm of wind (Matt.8:23–7) which was calculated to sink the ship and drown the occupants. Upon His being awakened, not by the raging wind or boisterous waves but by the agitated disciples, He rebuked the wind, telling it to be quiet, but not the waves.

When He delivered His discourse on the culminating events of the finale of the world's history, among His many arresting descriptions were those of heavenly signs involving the sun and the moon and the stars, and then he reverted to the turbulence that would agitate the earth: "Upon earth there would be distress of nations with perplexity; the sea and the waves roaring" (Luke 21:25). The picture, drawn in highly figurative language, is one of nations in distress with waves or rulers and politicians perplexed, that is literally without an answer. Satan is sometimes permitted to whip up the political climate and agitate the leaders.

In the voyage of life as delineated in the high drama of the current maritime story of Acts 27, Satan's design is made evident: nothing less than sending the ship to the bottom, and with it the world's most prestigious person, whose mission was to preach the Gospel in the heart of the Roman Empire and in the citadel of the imperial palace, but not if that wicked one could stop it. And he would do his utmost to foil the purpose of God. On this occasion his utmost was Euroclydon, and he came within an ace of succeeding (verse 14).

The elements were banded in an unholy conspiracy. The phraseology used is of the ship being caught, to which we might descriptively add "in the teeth of the gale" – from which one might just as well try to escape as from the mouth of a lion. Of the two, the latter would have been the easier.

Paul wrote to Timothy to warn those "who oppose them-selves, if God peradventure would give them repentance to the acknowledging of the truth; and that they may recover themselves out of the snare of the devil, who are taken captive by him at his will" (2Tim.2:25–6). Those addressed by opposing themselves had stood in their own light, and acted contrary to their own interests. In spite of the clear warning given authoritatively by the apostle, they had flouted it. And by so doing they had played into the hand of the wicked one, who was holding most of the aces and had napped their hand. Alternatively the wicked one, "who walketh about seeking whom he may devour" (1 Peter 5:8) had caught them napping. From then on the devil called the tune, the ship refused to answer to the helm, and would not even edge its way into Phenice. More gravely, the ship's bias was to the open sea, at which critical juncture the ship was given its head, and was equivalent to the devil taking over.

Satan's reputation is that of one who drives. Addiction of any kind of an evil nature is virtually a selling out to the wicked one, which was the recorded folly of King Ahab and his epitaph reads: "There was none like unto Ahab which did sell himself to work wickedness in the sight of the LORD, whom Jezebel his wife stirred up" (1 Kings 21:25). Mark the difference: Christ draws; the devil drives. Of Christ it is written, "When He putteth forth His sheep He goeth forth before them; He calleth His own sheep by name, and leadeth them out" (John 10:4). Before being expelled from the man at the tombs, the legion of devils besought Christ to send them into a large herd of swine feeding on the distant mountains. And, strange as it sounds, Christ acceded to their appeal, and upon their entering the browsing pigs, they ran pell-mell down a steep gradient and perished in the lake (Luke 8:32–3), probably driven by the ferocity of the devils.

This particular facet of the episode is a figure of temptation, leading to sin and that, in turn, to death, as described by James. It could aptly be said that James gives us the pedigree of sin. First of all there is the inner desire or lust which is appealed to by an external object to which it reaches out – or is drawn away – and clutches at the bait, thereby committing sin, or conceiving sin. It has been observed that sin is born big with death (John Wesley) which it in turn brings forth. Death is the logical corollary of sin (James 1:14–15). Exactly the same process was enacted in the fall of Judas – "And supper being ended, the devil having now put into the heart of Judas to betray Him" (John 13:2). The devil followed up his initial approach by a virtual takeover of the weakened Judas. And "when He had dipped the sop He gave it to Judas Iscariot the son of Simon, and after the sop Satan entered into him" (John 13: 26–7). "He then having received the sop went immediately out, and it was night" (John 13:30). Finally, in a vain endeavour to undo the treachery, he cast down the thirty pieces of silver in the Temple, and "went out and hanged himself" (Matt.27:5). Mark the steps from the first move to his final ruin: Satan planted the desire in his heart, later in the day he entered into him, and at that moment Judas became the willing tool of the Tempter and readily carried out the dastardly deed, and sin was conceived. A guilty conscience immediately tormented him, as it drove home the enormity of his crime. Despair overwhelmed him, and, with Satan at his elbow, drove him to self-murder. Perhaps weeks later they found his putrid corpse hanging from a tree, and when they cut him down, his body split open as it hit the ground, resulting in all his bowels gushing out (Acts 1:18).

The effects of the turbulence of the sea were lessened by sailing between Clauda and Crete and this respite allowed them to haul the trailing lifeboat on board. This boat's purpose was to take them from ship to shore when so required or to be used as a lifeboat in a crucial situation. Usually it was in the stern, and hidden from view. The violence of the tempest so threatened to pound it to pieces or the waves to overwhelm it and sink it that it was deemed necessary to haul it into the safety of the vessel.

There is a strong correspondence between the boat's purpose and people's religious convictions: never very apparent, but held in reserve, and seldom freely spoken of. Society in general does not usually wear its religious sentiments on its sleeve. Should life, however, take a turn for the worse, as in a serious illness or a domestic complication like the threatened break-up of a marriage or a financial crisis, religion is at hand to be used or appealed to. Somewhat like Abraham bringing Hagar into his household to shore up the tottering faith of himself and his spouse Sarah. To quote Harold Horton, "They had a Hagar behind the door, in case the promised child didn't materialise." For many people religion is mainly for storms and crises of life, especially does it come into its own when death is brooding over the family circle. And the mariners in the book of Jonah appear to give support to this view. A great wind of more than ordinary velocity, that threatened to break up the ship, so alarmed the sailors that they took out their gods and dusted them. To a man "they called upon them" (Jonah 1:5), not unlike those sailors in distress and at their wits' end spoken of in Psalm 107:28 – "They cry unto the LORD in their trouble, and He bringeth them out of their distress".

A concerted effort by the whole body of mariners to lift the boat wholesale out of the water onto the ship's deck had the appearance of a tug of war between them and the boisterous elements. The account says, "They had much work to come by the boat" (Acts 27:16), and eventually they succeeded. The moral it points to is of those who, after a lifetime of neglect, desperately call upon God. People who leave their praying and religious exercises until the crisis find it hard work indeed. Simon the ex-sorcerer, who was reproved by Simon Peter for offering him a bribe in exchange for power to impart the Holy Ghost to people, was charged "to pray to God that the thought of his heart might be forgiven". Simon's reaction was "Pray ye to the LORD for me, that none of these things ye have spoken come upon me" (Acts 8:22, 24). Charles Finney, who all his life had been a God-fearing but not a praying man, was alarmed when he began to seek God in all earnestness for forgiveness and salvation, but found he could not pray. To have a trailing religious persuasion is a far cry from possessing the essence of true religion in the heart, or the solid conviction of Paul, who could say, "For I am persuaded that neither death nor life, nor angels nor principalities nor powers, nor things present, nor things to come, nor height, nor depth, nor any other creature shall be able to separate us from the love of God, which is in Christ Jesus our LORD" (Rom.8:38–9). James, in his searching appraisal, hits the nail on the head with his epitome of true religion: "If any man among you seem to be religious, and bridleth not his tongue, but deceiveth his own heart, this man's religion is vain. Pure religion and undefiled before God and the Father is this, to visit the fatherless and widows in their affliction, and to keep himself unspotted from the world" (James 1:26, 27), "the essence of which is to minister comfort, counsel and relief to those who need it most, in their most helpless and hopeless state, and to keep oneself from the maxims, tempers and customs of this world. This cannot be done until we have given our hearts to God and love our neighbour as ourselves" (John Wesley).

Those who wait for the storms of life before they do this will have indeed "much work to come by the boat" (Acts 27:16, 17).

* * * * * * * * * * * * * * * * * * * *

SERMON 6

'HELPS'

Acts 27:17: *They used helps undergirding the ship.*

'Helps' have been defined as those who have a peculiar dexterity to succour or assist people in distress or need. This sentiment is summed up by the man of Macedonia, who appeared to Paul by night in a vision while he waited at Troas to receive from God his next assignment, for it seemed that the apostle had come to a cul-de-sac, but not for long as the Macedonian's appeal to come over and help them. This was as clear a directive as could be wished for. The Macedonian's invitation was an admission of need and Paul had the heart and ability to alleviate that need. The place helps in the catalogue of ministries features in the letter to the Corinthians is inserted between gifts of healing and governments. This lends support to the idea that there are those who exercise particular gifts in a specific manner rather than as general helpers (1 Cor.12:28).

The grain ship of Alexandria, in which Paul was being carried under guard to Rome, was being battered by tempestuous waves and hurricane-force winds. Its creaking boards were giving notice of intense strain. After safely hauling the lifeboat on board the sailors concentrated on strengthening the timbers by re-enforcing the hull with special ropes provided for such emergencies – a technique known as frapping. The ropes would be cast around the hull and tightened by winches to keep the planks together. Presumably they would have been threaded beneath rather than around the hull, and were thus said to undergird the ship. Aptly they were called 'helps', for they helped to keep the planks from

31

separating under the severe buffeting of the more than gale-force winds.

There are several lessons connoted in the usage of the gear called 'helps', and these are comparable to the ministry of helps cited in First Corinthians chapter twelve. Helps supplement other ministries which are more honourable or prominent and possessing a higher proficiency in their normal function. But seasons of emergency call for their usefulness to be supplemented. A classical example was demonstrated in the drama of the crucifixion of Christ. A little before the striking of the ninth hour, the LORD cried "I thirst!" whereupon a soldier took a sponge and after filling it with vinegar, put it on a reed and held it up to Christ to drink (Matt.27:48). As soon as He drank the proffered liquid "He gave up the ghost". It was the sponge that supplied the means of satisfying His thirst, but it was the reed that supplied the extension enabling the drink to reach the lips of the sufferer. Its ministry supplemented the succour of the contents of the sponge container and played the part of an indispensable 'help'.

Paul likened the church at Corinth to a ploughed and cultivated field and called it "God's husbandry" (1 Cor.3:9). It was he who had ploughed and harrowed the land before sowing it with the good seed of the Word of God. Later, Apollos came to Corinth and "mightily convinced the Jews, showing by the Scriptures that Jesus was Christ". His ministry is said to have "helped them much which had believed by grace" (Acts 18:27–8). The Gentile believers had received the grace of God through the preaching of Paul; but the Jews were convinced through the powerful Bible expositions of Apollos, a disciple of John the Baptist, whose want of a fuller knowledge of Christ was supplied by Aquila and Priscilla, after hearing him speak in the synagogue at Corinth (Acts 18:26). His ministry to the Church subsequent to his own conversion was that of watering the field that Paul had cultivated. Apollos' use of the 'watering can' was as proficient as Paul's had been in using the plough and broadcasting the seed.

The terminology 'helps' conveys a broad classification inclusive of a variant of ministries ranging from the ministerial and practical to the governmental or judicial. Their place in the list of ministries compiled in the letter to the Corinthians lies between that of healings and that of governments. Surprisingly, John Mark, whose beginning in the Christian ministry was very shaky, so graduated, that from his Roman prison Paul singled out the nephew of Barnabas as one whose ministry would be profitable to the apostle, and charges Timothy to bring him to Rome. To minister to an apostle or for an apostle was no mean thing, and he who had blotted his escutcheon by defecting from the post of duty when a companion of Paul and Barnabas, had so enhanced his reputation as to become a 'help' to the apostle to the Gentiles. A companion of Paul's, especially in the closing years of his life and itinerary, was Luke, called the beloved physician and almost certainly the one whom the apostle refers to as "the brother whose praise is in the Gospel throughout all the churches" (2 Cor.8:18). When associates were forsaking the apostle like rats from a doomed ship, the writer of the third Gospel stuck to him like a limpet. "Only Luke is with me" were among the last words he ever penned (2 Tim.4:11). No better service could Lucius the Church historian have rendered to the apostle than putting on record the extraordinary achievements of the pioneer of the Gentile churches.

Titus, too, must rank as one of the mighties of the opening of the Gospel era. A succinct compliment paid to him by the citizen of Tarsus, designated no mean city, was "that in all their tribulations, he was filled with comfort and exceedingly joyful. For when we were come to Macedonia our flesh had no rest but we were troubled on every side; without were fightings, within were fears. Nevertheless, God that comforteth those that are cast down, comforted us by the coming of Titus" (2 Cor.7:6). Literally, the word comfort means 'with strength'. Paul was buttressed by the words of comfort and consolation of his junior colleague and fellow labourer. Jonathan had exercised a like ministry towards David when he visited him in the wood called Hachilah, and "strengthened his hand in God" (1 Sam.23:16). These were shades of Moses' action in the battle of Rephidim (Exodus 17:12–13). Moses interceded for Israel on a hill overlooking the battlefield, symbolised by his holding his hands heavenward. As long as his hands were held up, Israel prevailed, but when he grew weary and lowered them Amalek prevailed. Observing the problem with Moses, Aaron and Hur came to his help and, together, steadied his arms by holding them up on either side for the remainder of the day, and Israel defeated the invaders and altogether prevailed. Moses' weary arms had been undergirded by two colleagues whose names "Aaron and Hur are symbols of a very high degree of holiness" (R. Colley). Saul lost his kingdom because he was flagrantly remiss in carrying out the express battle orders of God to slay en masse the inveterate enemies of God's people, against whom God had declared perpetual war in wrath without mixture (Exodus 17:16). Jonathan, Saul's son, strengthened the hands of David, Saul's successor, who would carry out what his father had lamentably failed to do, viz. crush the Amalekites beyond recovery. David's drooping arms of faith would be stimulated and his courage reinvigorated by a rerun of his unprecedented victory over Goliath the giant, whose loudmouthed braggadocio had sent shivers down the spines of Saul and Abner as well as down those of the entire Israeli army. Jonathan did invaluable service to the cause of God the day he sought David in the wood of Hachilah and helped him recover his moral strength.

A further lesson gleaned from the helps used to undergird the battered grain ship from threatened disintegration, was of the covert nature of their function. The necessity of having to draw them under the hull meant they were out of sight. More than one deed of valour has been enacted in the glare of publicity, but true courage neither needs nor desires an audience in the performance of what amounted to more than duty or of what was expected of them, because its incentive is the good of being and not personal glory. Like the anchor of hope, the ropes were taut and holding weakened planks together while being out of sight.

Speaking of the Christian hope the writer states, "Which hope we have as an anchor of the soul both sure and steadfast", which is a reference to the two barbs on the conventional anchor, which grip the marl on the seabed. But the figurative anchor of hope is cast above "within the veil or Holy of Holies" (Heb.6:18–19). Paul wrote, "Hope that is seen is not hope, but if we hope for that which we see not, then do we with patience wait for it" (Rom.8:24, 25). True hope is the anticipation of future good, and is always something beyond the ability of natural acumen to perceive. An anchor, therefore, is only doing its work of holding a ship and preventing it from drifting, when it is in the seabed and out of sight.

Likewise true helps avoid publicity. John the Baptist, Christ's herald, disclaimed all credit and engaged no public relations officer. The Jews sent priests and Levites from Jerusalem to ask John who he was. They worded their enquiry in such a way that it had a strong appeal to the ego as they asked, "What sayest thou of thyself?" John in a few clipped sentences retorted, "I am the voice of one crying in the wilderness. Prepare ye the way of the LORD, make His path straight" (John 1:22–3).

Ropes are very ordinary things and have no singular attraction. They are spun from hemp, with nothing highly technical about them. Nevertheless, there are situations which arise in which the rope is the best, if not the only answer. A case in point is of Jeremiah's timely rescue from the dungeon in the court of the prison at Jerusalem. His rescuer was Ebed-melech, an Ethiopian eunuch aided by thirty men who had successfully interceded on his behalf to Zedekiah the king. Using no elaborate tackle but cords and a bundle of old rags to cushion their pressure under Jeremiah's arms, the operation was efficiently carried out (Jer.35:13).

In the list of ministerial gifts drawn up in the Corinthian epistle, helps are placed between gifts of healings and governments, and comprise prestigious names like apostles, prophets, teachers, miracles and gifts of healings, but helps have a nondescript classification. Notwithstanding, their usage has avoided many a parlous situation, as in the current story narrated in Acts 27. A deeply laid plot to waylay the apostle by more than forty would-be assassins, under the pretext of having him brought from the castle to the Jewish Council for further questioning, was only prevented by the quick action of Paul's anonymous nephew. In the providence of God he learned of the plot and hastened to the castle to divulge it to his uncle. Paul, in turn, called for a centurion to take his nephew to Claudius Lysias, the Roman Tribune, who revealed the plot to the commanding officer. Within hours, under heavily armed escort, Paul was on his way to Cæsarea, to the safety of Felix's headquarters. Under God, Paul's nephew was the length of rope that saved Paul's life that night. One dares to suggest that there was not another individual that would have risked carrying that top secret information to the chief captain on that occasion. Had it leaked out, the courageous young man would not have survived the reprisals of an enraged but foiled body of religious fanatics.

Help not infrequently comes from unexpected sources and in unpredictable ways that convey a strong tang of the divine about them. In hot pursuit of the woman who had given birth to the man-child destined to rule all nations with a rod of iron and to strip the devil or serpent of his usurped dominion over the kingdoms of the world, the dragon casts out of his mouth a flood of water to overwhelm her. Unexpectedly the earth comes to the help of the woman, and opens its mouth to swallow up the flood that the dragon had cast out of its mouth, so that the biter was bitten; the devourer's invective was devoured. Ordinarily, the earth is an accomplice of the enemy of God and His people, and is designated 'the god of this world', yet the woman, alias the Church, the true

Israel of God, is delivered by help from an alien quarter. The imagery of the episode was anticipated in the dramatic event of Jonathan's rescue from the unreasonable oath of Saul his father, who without compunction, was prepared to carry out the death sentence for innocent violation of the oath. His deliverance came by the people who loudly vociferated against the proposed execution, and figuratively swallowed up his rage, and as the earth had helped the woman, so the people helped and delivered the young hero (1 Sam.14:4–5).

An unlikely means of deliverance from death is a strand of wool. Consternation arose when upon their completing a tall chimneystack, the workmen removed the scaffolding and the operation was carried out with one of the workforce remaining at the top of the stack to facilitate a difficult task. Normal practice was that of leaving a rope behind to lower himself to the ground. A large crowd had gathered looking up anxiously – they had forgotten to leave the rope. The poor man, greatly agitated, was walking around the very narrow ledge at the top of the stack, and was threatening to jump off, which meant certain death. Someone had sent for his wife, who called, "John!", and calmed him, and then directed him to unravel the worsted, that is his woollen socks. Ingeniously she told him to let the long woollen thread down, weighted with a fragment of dried mortar, while he held the other end. As soon as the end which dangled by the piece of mortar was caught by a workman a length of cord was attached to it, and the woman called out and told him to pull the strand of wool up and secure the cord. No sooner was the cord secured than a rope was fastened to it and again the workman was instructed to haul up the rope by the cord. Then the anxious man secured the rope around the ridge at the top of the stack. Within minutes he lowered himself down by the rope, and upon reaching the bottom of the stack threw himself into the arms of his waiting wife and amidst his sobs could be heard crying, "O, Mary, thou hast saved my life!" A length of unravelled wool from his worsted socks, and the calmness of a level-headed woman, had been his lifeline or his life. It was an unlikely means indeed, but it secured the desired end.

By undergirding, the ship was strengthened where it was most needed. "For if the foundations be destroyed what can the righteous do?" (Psalm 11:3). The bottom of a ship is the most exposed part of the hull, especially with the unseen dangers of the ocean, such as hidden rocks and quicksands, and the importance of re-enforcing the ship's lower timbers can easily be seen. When ships spring a leak it is always below the waterline, the ill-fated *Titanic* being the supreme example. In spite of its double steel hull, the ship was ripped open below the waterline by the submerged section of the iceberg that sealed its doom. It was claimed to be unsinkable but the providence of God, out of whose womb comes the ice, proved differently. Isaiah counselled, "Trust ye in the LORD forever; for in the LORD Jehovah is everlasting strength" (Isaiah 26:4).

* * * * * * * * * * * * * * * * * * * *

SERMON 7

AVOIDING THE QUICKSANDS

Acts 27:17: *...and fearing lest they should fall into the quicksand, strake sail, and so were driven.*

Just in time the sailors remembered the quicksands which can sometimes present a far greater danger than rocks, as great a hazard as they to ships and seafarers. Quicksands lie below the surface of the sea, while by and large dangerous rocks project well above the water level. Disaster is virtually certain if a boat ploughs into the quicksands. It is held as firmly as if in a vice, and presents a sitting-duck target to violent waves, which cause the craft to break up quickly. Paul's warning was already beginning to bite as he had previously averred, "I perceive that this voyage will be with hurt and much damage, not only of the lading and of the ship, but also of our lives." Their ignoring Paul's warning amounted to disdaining God, from whom the apostle had received the gale warning. And their contempt of heaven's weather lore would cost them dearly.

Death has always been God's ultimate penalty for disobedience. Adam's turning a deaf ear to God's warning merited the maximum punishment: "In the day thou eatest thereof – of the tree of the knowledge of good and evil – thou shalt surely die" (Gen.2:17). God's inexorable rule is "For the wages of sin is death, but the gift of God is eternal life through Jesus Christ our LORD" (Rom.6:23). There is much more, however, in the warning than meets the eye. Holy writ refers to a second death, which devolves upon all impenitent sinners, whose names are missing from the Book of Life, which is the final arbiter. "John saw the dead – of all ages – small and great, stand before God, which was made possible by the sea giving up the dead which were in it; and death and hell delivered up the dead which were in them; Death gave up the bodies of men; Hades was the receptacle of separate souls to be reunited to their bodies, finally to be cast into the lake of fire, no more to be separated, because their names were not found written in the Book of Life" (John Wesley commentating on Revelation 20:13–15). An interesting sidelight on that statement is that of Paul's assertion in the epistle to the Philippians that the names of Clement, with other of his fellow labourers, were in the Book of Life (Phil.4:3). His speaking with such confidence provokes the thought that a revelation of the catalogue of names found in that closed book had been granted during the season of his "being caught up to the third heaven and heard such things that it was not lawful for him to utter" (2 Cor.12:2–5).

When John the Baptist sounded out the warning in the desert of Judæa "to flee from the wrath to come" (Luke 3:7), uppermost in his mind would have been the wrath of the Romans against Jerusalem's stubborn resistance during the siege of AD 70. It is stated in "Josephus' Wars" that at the fall of the city tens of thousands were slaughtered and that many of them were crucified in such huge numbers that the executioners ran out of timber. Far worse, however, is the wrath to be poured out on the world by the seven angels from their seven bowls pungently delineated in the sixteenth chapter of the Revelation; yet, as horrific as that is, it is only to be paled into insignificance by the wrath of the lake of fire, called the second death at the end of the world, and climax of human history (Rev.20:12–15). Because the final judgement is at the end of the world and remotely futuristic, it is out of sight, and with the massive majority it is out of mind, for the uncountable majority "mind earthly things" (Phil.3:19). Only the fear generated by the nearness of death fills people with alarm and when accompanied by the imminence of the Judgement Day, brings them to a stand. Jonah's forty-day preaching itinerary in the city of Nineveh, and his relentless message: "Forty days and Nineveh shall be destroyed" produced a citywide revival and repentance. From the least to the greatest, the entire population, young and old, the cattle included, were draped in sackcloth, "for king and people believed God" (Jonah 3:5).

In the quicksands is mirrored the judgement and wrath of God. Elihu brought Job to his senses by a solemn reminder of eschatological realities; not the least of which is the judgement of God. His words to the patriarch and his friends were, "Because there is wrath beware, lest He take thee away with His stroke: then a great ransom cannot deliver thee" (Job 36:18).

In his opening speech, Elihu had enlarged upon the value and virtue of the ransom provided by God for anyone who shall pray, "I have sinned and perverted that which was right, and it profited me not; He will deliver his soul from going into the pit, and his life shall see the light. Lo, all these things worketh God oftentimes with man, to bring back his soul from the pit, to be lightened with the light of the living" (Job 33:27–30).

Let the ship, though, once find itself in the quicksands, and there is no answer. God's ransom provided in Christ by His redemptive sacrifice is no longer effective. At the bar of heavenly justice there is no further forgiveness at the final assize of God, rather His wrath is poured out of the cup of His indignation, without mixture. Its justice is pure and unalloyed without mercy (Rev.14:10).

Not without meaning is Christ's summing up of His sermon on the mount, where the duty of a Christian is clearly set forth, which could well be described as Christ's manifesto of the Kingdom of Heaven (Matthew, chapters 5 to 7). Of that unique discourse, the final statement contains the warning on the package: "Everyone who heareth these sayings of Mine, and doeth them not, shall be likened unto a foolish man which built his house upon the sand: and the rain descended, and the winds blew and beat upon that house: and great was the fall of it" (Matt.7:26–7). The analogy can hardly be missed between the ship on the quicksands pounded by the waves and winds until its final break-up: and the house on the sand swept away by the relentless battering by the rain and floods and wind of God's judgement. Great was the fall of both: the ship never to be salvaged, the house never to be rebuilt.

Elihu further opined, "Lest He take thee away with His stroke" (Job 36:18). One thrust from the sharp two-edged sword proceeding from His mouth (Rev.2:16; 19:21), and millions will be banished to the lake of fire with His word of enacted justice reverberating in their ears: "Depart from Me ye cursed into everlasting fire prepared for the devil and his angels" (Matt.25:41; 20:10).

Impending disaster stirs people to resort to any device to avoid or ward it off. Apprised of the relentless march of Joshua's victorious army, and aware that within a little their city Gibeon would be swept away, the Gibeons resorted to the strategy of subterfuge. A deputation was hastily despatched in the guise of ambassadors from a distant state, who were desirous of making a non-aggression treaty with them. So plausible was their story and deceptive their disguise that Joshua and the elders were tricked into making the requested treaty. Three days later Joshua learned of the deception and condemned the men of Gibeon to perpetual servitude, but Gibeon and its inhabitants were spared. As costly as their deceit was, it substantiated the aphorism of Solomon that "a living dog is better than a dead lion".

With Euroclydon driving hard, it was essential to retard the ship's motion, if it was possible. One thing within their power was to strake or lower the mainsail. A sail's purpose is to enable the boat to move forward, and prevent it from being becalmed, like many people who are ambitious to get on in the world, to avoid getting into a rut. Baruch, the private secretary of Jeremiah, was no exception. His partnership with Jeremiah was detrimental to his chances of public recognition or promotional prospects to governmental office. His brother was well on his way to the top socially and civically, but the prophet's scribe was becalmed in the doldrums. Knowing the unvoiced sentiments of Baruch, the Lord pointedly questioned him, "Seekest thou great things for thyself?" and before he could collect his wits together to reply, God gave him counsel that indicated his awareness of his ambition – that of the glory of human greatness – and bluntly charged Baruch in the briefest of counsels: "Seek them not", then gave as the reason that the top jobs in the government would soon be non-existent, because God would bring evil upon all flesh: the king and his courtiers and his subjects (Jer.45:5). But despite the tragedy of the nation's early removal to an alien land and the denudation of Jerusalem, his own life would be spared, and, as it were, "be given him for a prey".

Every man on board, from the captain and shipowner, not excluding Julian the military officer, to the soldiers and ship's crew and company were eager to get to the next port, estimated to be about forty miles further along the coast of Crete, and eventually unload their rich and welcome cargo of grain at the nearest port. With a sense of relief they would have hoisted the mainsail to the friendly south wind, but a ferocious north-easter had taken over, and to return to the despised safe haven was impossible. Not for nothing does it say "they were driven". Their perilous situation called for a slowing down. With the mainsail bellied out to the straining of the canvas, they could easily keel over. Involuntarily, the seamen lowered it, which in effect was like applying the brake.

God's charge to men is that they should "humble themselves under His mighty hand, that He might exalt them in due time" (1 Pet.5:6). A similar directive is given by James in James 5:10. All glorying other than in God is highly objectionable, as instinct in definitive advice found in Jeremiah's writing: "Thus saith the Lord, let not the wise man glory in his wisdom; neither let the mighty man glory in his might; let not the rich man glory in his riches: but let him that glorieth glory in this that he understandeth and knoweth Me, that I am the Lord, which exercises loving kindness, judgement and righteousness in the earth: For in these things I delight, saith the LORD" (Jer.9:23–4).

Paul's instructions to the church at Philippi were, among other things, that nothing was to be done which was animated either by strife or vainglory. No believer is to contend for mastery over a fellow believer; rather he is told in lowliness of mind to esteem another better than himself, which is counter to the spirit of vainglory or love of praise, the secret of which is allowing the mind which is in Christ to be ruling within the heart "who became obedient to death, even the death of the cross" (Phil.2:3–5, 8). Neither is it possible to humble oneself lower than that.

Isaac is an outstanding example of one who did not strive for masteries. Rather than contend for Abram's wells, which the Philistines had filled in, yet his servants had re-dug, he removed to leave the Philistines in possession. The first well was Esek, meaning 'contention', and the second Sitnah, signifying 'hatred'. Meekly he withdrew to allow the Philistines a free hand, but God immediately compensated him, by his servants striking water yet again. Aptly the new well was called Rehoboth, meaning 'room', his comment upon which was "God hath made room for us, and we shall be fruitful in the land" (Gen.26:22).

Zacchaeus was brought down to earth in more ways than one during the LORD'S final journey to Jerusalem, which took him through Jericho, and was enacted on the exit road from the 'City of Palm Trees'. Oddly, the scenario was displayed not in a palm tree, for which Jericho was famous, but in a sycamore, whose thick foliage gave ample cover to the commissioner of the tax office. He desired a close-up look at Christ, from a concealed vantage point, and the close relative of the fig tree was ideal. His status among the publicans was that of the crest. He was chief among them and his salary would have been in the top bracket. With such credentials he could well take a little scorn – not uncommon against publicans – in his stride. He was riding on the crest of a wave, with his sails fully unfurled, until the particular event of Christ's journey took him over the stretch of the road where the sycamore tree arched the way. No one was more surprised than Zacchaeus when the LORD looked up and spoke to him, and called upon him by name to come down quickly. Without more ado he answered to his name and obeyed with haste; thereupon, although not asked, he gave away what must have been his large savings in one single benevolent gesture. In so doing he had not only come down from the tree, but had come down in his own estimation and this could be figuratively compared with the lowering of the mainsail.

Notwithstanding the lowered sail, the vessel continued to be driven by the wind without abatement. Many people, too late, have discovered that having made a wrong decision, it is not easy to turn back on one's tracks or even reduce the momentum. Such wrong decisions, especially moral ones, are not easily righted, and the journey of life confirms the sentiment. Everywhere along the sea-coast of life are the eyesores and heartbreaks of those who have parted with a good conscience and made shipwreck of faith (1 Tim.1:19) because of a first step of wilful disobedience, like many who refused to believe that the first 'fix' would ere long lead to their being hooked. When the pigs ran down the steep slope of Gadara under the impetus of the evil spirits who had taken possession of them, and came to the cliff, they discovered too late that their momentum had so developed that they could not stop and were hurtled into the sea to perish (Luke 8:32–3).

Of King Ahab the sacred historian wrote, "There was none like him who sold himself to work wickedness in the sight of the LORD, whom Jezebel his wife stirred up" (1 Kings 21:25). Elijah reported to him in his final encounter he had with him in the embezzled vineyard of Naboth, that the very ground which had soaked up Naboth's blood through his brutal murder and mischievous indictment of his noble neighbour, that there would the dogs lick up his blood as they had the murdered owner (1 Kings 21:19). Worse even, was the tailpiece of the report, that God would prematurely "cut off all his posterity" (1 Kings 19:21), and for the first time in his murky reign, the fear of God so wrought upon him that he lowered his mainsail and humbled himself: he exchanged the canvas for sackcloth, and lay on the ground. In Bible verbiage it says "he went softly" or in deep humility. Consistent with the divine principle, that "God will exalt the humble, but the proud He knoweth afar off" and impressed with the wicked king's sincerity, He mitigated the severity of the sentence, declaring, "Because Ahab had humbled himself, the judgement would not fall in his days, but be postponed to his son's day" (1 Kings 3:21–9).

The architect of Ahab's wicked career was a pernicious and pagan wife who is charged with stirring him up. Her spiritual counterpart, also called Jezebel, and who was prominent in the Asian church of Thyatira, was a self-styled prophetess, and had been given full liberty to teach. In exercising this ministry she had "seduced God's servants in persuading them to commit fornication, and to eat things sacrificed to idols" (Rev.2:20). Women in the Bible are often representative of false doctrines, which in turn are likened to crosswinds (Ephes.4:14). And all who are tossed about by false doctrines are compared with children or immature Christians, and so are easily seduced. Jezebel was the wind of evil intent that stirred up Ahab to commit malicious acts against God's children and prophets. In spite, however, of Ahab's reformation, he was again driven by the 450 prophets of the groves, all of whom were sponsored by Jezebel, and persuaded, against the warning of Micaiah, one of the few surviving prophets of the LORD, to buckle on his armour and engage Benhadad in battle, to recover Ramoth Gilead, wrongfully in the possession of the Syrian king. Just as Paul had warned the Roman centurion to remain in the security of the Fair Havens and not to venture out to sea, so after Micaiah's warning of Ahab being a fatal casualty if he went to battle, the words proved to be no scarecrow but were fully confirmed. Ahab rashly engaged his forces with those of Jehoshaphat against the army of Syria, and his chariot became his hearse.

There is a striking moral enforced in the story of the tempest that mercilessly battered the grain ship of Alexandria, a mere cork on the waves off the Cretian coast, for fourteen days and nights, which is four times emphasised in Psalm 107 concerning those in desperate trouble at the four corners of the compass: "Then they cried unto the LORD in their trouble, and He delivered them out of all their distresses" (Psalm 107:6, 13, 19, 28).

* * * * * * * * * * * * * * * * * * * *

SERMON 8

ALL HANDS ON DECK

Acts 27:18–19: *And we being exceedingly tossed with a tempest, the next day they lightened the ship; and the third, day we cast out with our hands the tackling of the ship.*

Far from there being any let-up in the fury of the gale, the storm became even more tempestuous. Like a cork on the wave, the ship was being tossed about alarmingly. To such straits were they reduced that they resorted to action only taken as a last measure: they lightened the ship, throwing overboard first the least valuable of the cargo.

When death draws uncomfortably near, material things lose their value, even as Christ intimated in His reproof to a greedy brother, who wanted the LORD to apply pressure to a brother who had by the law of seniority inherited the family estate, in order to his receiving a share. How trivial are the concerns of men when compared with Christ's mission to this world, which was to seek lost sinners and save them from the pit of perdition. Instead of complying with the man's request, the LORD roundly reproved him and afterwards charged the crowd of onlookers saying, "Take heed and beware of covetousness: for man's life consisteth not in the abundance of the things which he possesseth" (Luke 12:15). With heavy seas rolling over the gunwale it was essential that the ship should disgorge its superfluities in order to keep her well above the water level.

A sense of danger will revalue our priorities more than anything else. Life displaces any other factor in the matter of priorities, and brings into focus Christ's observation: "All that a man hath will he give for his life". When a ship is sinking at sea the natural instinct of all on board is to save their lives. As the last lifeboat was about to draw away from the doomed ship, a man amongst those left behind cried – naming a large sum of money – for a place in the boat. There were no acceptors. How true is the proverb: "A living dog is better than a dead lion" or in the New Testament setting, "Lazarus the beggar in Paradise was the envy of the rich man in hell" (Luke 16:19– 24).

It was strange indeed that they delayed jettisoning their excess baggage (sometimes called hindering superfluities) until the following day. Perhaps they were gambling on a radical change in the weather by the next day. If so, it was mere wishful thinking. Human experience has confirmed that delays can be dangerous. When the buried city of Herculaneum was dug out of the lava with which it had been overwhelmed, a man was found collecting valuables from a house but both were entombed before he could get clear of the stream of molten lava bearing down upon the city. He had gambled high stakes to enrich himself, but he lost the lottery. A far more serious act of folly is that of procrastination in the issue of the soul's salvation. Sadly, millions are blameworthy of that enormous folly, and mistakenly think, 'There is always tomorrow'.

Of all tempests there is none more alarming than the tempest of a guilty conscience, which has much in common with the sting of a scorpion. Unnatural or supernatural locusts are seen emerging in dense clouds from the bottomless pit after one described as "a star fallen from heaven had opened it with the key he was carrying, upon the sounding of the fifth trumpet alias the first woe" (Rev.9:1–3). Their instructions were to torment but not slay those men not sealed in their foreheads by the Spirit of God, which is synonymous with the apostle's warning: "Now if any man have not the Spirit of Christ he is none of His" (Rom.8:9). So painful is the sting of these grotesque creatures that it is compared with "the sting of a scorpion when he striketh a man" (Rev.9:5).

Enlarging upon the excruciating pain, the writer declared that "in those days shall men seek death and shall not find it, and shall desire to die, and death shall flee from them" (Rev.9:6). Death, which may aptly be compared to those gorbellied monsters the locusts – all mouth and belly – will flee from devouring humans, under God's prohibition

Jeremiah compared the wicked to the troubled sea, which cannot rest, constantly casting up mire and dirt. Identical to this is the inner monitor called conscience when under a deep sense of guilt, upon its being stirred up by the Holy Ghost, whose prime function is, "to convince the world of sin, of righteousness and of judgement (John 16:11–17). Nothing less than this was responsible for the terrified reaction of Felix the Roman Governor of Judæa to Paul's dissertation of the Christian faith after being summoned to appear before him. At that interview Paul "reasoned of righteousness, temperance and of judgement to come", after which Paul's judge visibly trembled in the company of his wife, having been greatly wrought upon by his guilty conscience. Righteousness and temperance were alien to his unjust and immoral character (Acts 24:24–5). Judge though he were, the thought of his standing before the bar of God "the blessed and only Potentate, the King of kings and LORD of lords; who only hath immortality, dwelling in the light which no man can approach unto; whom no man hath seen nor can see" (1 Tim.6:15–16), was of all terrors the most unnerving.

A tempestuous sea "lifts a boat up to the heavens one moment and drops it into the depths the next" (Psalm 107:26). So the guilt-ridden conscience tosses the guilty one alternately from hope to despair like the terror of the nondescript locusts of Revelation chapter 9. Conscience has driven men to such despair, Judas being the supreme example, as to incite them to take a hasty departure from this life, only to discover that they have jumped out of one fire into a far hotter one, through a yet greater deception on Satan's part. Some have been saved from casting themselves over the precipice of self-murder only by providential intervention. Jeremiah spoke of the troubled sea casting up mire and dirt, just as the Spirit of God disturbs the false peace within the breasts of the guilty party by setting all its sins in array before it, as in the case of the terrified Roman Governor Felix. Anyone who has dealt personally with individuals who have fallen into deep sin will have perceived the great torment of mind. The only remedy is a full and frank confession to the party concerned, as when a man has betrayed his partner's confidence in him and has associated illicitly with someone else's wife.

Indisputably the antidote is drastic: he must confess his infidelity to the partner of his bosom as well as to the LORD; then his tempestuous sea will become a great calm. There is no other remedy. Much grace is required to do this, but the willing and trembling delinquent will prove that God is the God of all grace and the Father of mercy.

A still further worsening of their peril stimulated the crew to adopt yet more drastic measures following their dumping of their cargo of the previous day. They now cut down the masts, which were serving no useful purpose due to the intensity of the storm; and to assist in this arduous work all on board were co-opted. Luke, in his narrative, changes the personal pronoun from 'they' to 'we' averring, "We cast out with our own hands the tackling of the ship" (verse 19). Passengers and prisoners, as well as soldiers and seamen, concertedly pulled their weight to keep the ship on an even keel. A common danger unites people who otherwise have little or nothing in common. When a nation is at war, political parties of every colour sink their differences and unite to combat the common foe. Their common weal eclipses all their differences. When Israel invaded the land of promise the seven ethnic nationalities, of whom the Canaanites were the predominant, closed ranks to repel the common foe. Before this they were at war with one another. The same conduct can historically be seen with the north American Indians and African tribes coming together at such times when before they had been raiding each other's territory and slaughtering one another. Herod and Pilate had little room for each other and were decidedly lacking in amity, but their antipathy against Christ was the means of bringing them together to a friendly relationship. On the day of the crucifixion they patched up their differences, as it is written: "On the same day, Pilate and Herod were made friends together, for before they were at enmity between themselves" (Luke 23:12).

If the winds of terror or the winds of change for the worse come howling through the cordage then there will be few protests about parting with the tackling of the ship so to speak. If there is even only a slender chance of the feared danger or serious loss to health or reputation can be averted then such tactics will be accepted. Christ said to Paul as he lay in the dust on the Damascus road, "Saul, Saul why persecutes thou Me? It is hard for thee to kick against the pricks." Paul's mind was in turmoil. The ox goad of a guilty conscience was stabbing him acutely, and when told to get up and proceed to an address in Straight Street in the city he obeyed like a docile lamb (Acts 9:4–9). Hours before, he had been snorting out his rage like a dragon against the Church of Christ. Now totally subdued, he meekly enquired of the LORD what should he do to escape from the storm raging in his conscience. He was ready to take his marching orders from the Christ he had persecuted so savagely, but whom he now addressed as LORD.

Years later, when he reminisced on the traumatic nature of his conversion, he said, "What things were gain to me, those I counted loss for Christ." For three days he waited in literal bodily darkness and still greater darkness of mind, until Ananias, who was instructed by the LORD, appeared and laid his hands upon him, to receive his sight "and immediately there fell from his eyes what appeared to be scales" (Acts 9:18– 19).

An able commentator has noted that the words used by Paul of "gain and loss" (Phil.3:7), which he gladly parted with to receive salvation, through the righteousness of Christ received by faith alone, in the Greek, signify the loss sustained at sea in a storm, when goods are thrown overboard for the sake of saving the ship and the people on board. The passage has been paraphrased as if the apostle had said, "In making the voyage of life, for the sake of gaining salvation, I proposed to purchase it with my circumcision, and my care in observing the ritual and moral precepts of the Law; and I put a great value on those things on account of the gain or advantage I was to make by them, but when I became a Christian I willingly threw them overboard, as of no value in purchasing salvation, and this I did for the sake of gaining salvation through faith in Christ as my only Saviour" (Dr Macknight).

Not only did Paul cast away all that he gloried in as a self-righteous Pharisee, but with hindsight viewed them as dung, both worthless and odious, as the putrescent excrements of a man or animal. "The Greek word signifies the vilest refuse of things, such as the dregs of liquors, the dross of metals, the excrements of animals, the most worthless scraps of meat, the basest of offals fit only for dogs. He that loses all things not excepting himself, gains Christ, and is gained by Christ" (John Wesley).

Put in another way, Paul viewed his conscientious obedience to the Law of Moses and his slavish performance of the ceremony and ritual pertaining thereto as worthless in securing salvation or heaven. Actually he saw them as obstacles to his voyage to heaven and readily jettisoned them as one would contraband at the approach of customs officials, who were coming to search the holds, with strong suspicions of illicit cargo. Time was when Paul had been inordinately proud of his Pharisaical trappings, and high standard of personal righteousness, but the terrifying storm of a guilty conscience and censure of the Holy Ghost that had produced such disquietude of mind convinced him that until his moral assets, as he thought, were flung overboard with disdain if not disgust, he would never make the port of Heaven (Phil.3:7–9).

Luke's relation of the episode lays stress on the usage of their hands, stating, "We cast out with our own hands" (verse 19). To live without hands is virtually impossible. Solomon's original description of the body with his usage of graphic imagery singles the hands out as the keepers of the body, and during the season of old age subject to trembling (Eccles.12:3). Attempts at threading a needle with trembling hands always lead to frustration, but under normal conditions what Trojan service they render. It is likewise important to remember that hands are responsible for almost everything that is made. Machinery gets more and more complicated and sophisticated, but the tools which make the machinery were made by hands.

Character, however, is the product of faith in the achievements of Christ's hands. When those hands were pinioned to a cross, they procured man's salvation from sin and death and hell. Isaiah had such in mind when he quoted God as saying, "Behold, I have graven thee upon the palms of My hands" (Isaiah 49:16), which has been likened to those who inscribe a name upon their hand, as a reminder of some service to be rendered to them or a duty to be performed for them. Engravings are often wrought on a hard surface or metal plate with an engraving iron. Figuratively the nails in Christ's hands were the irons that pierced Him that we might be indelibly fixed in His mind. For this reason Christ showed His disbelieving disciples His hands and His feet, which were incontestable proofs of His identity and, more importantly, evidences of His love and constant remembrance of them.

Hands always speak of service, but no service rendered to God nor any sacrifice we make for Him can atone for our sins. Nothing but the blood of Christ can procure the goodwill of God with the glory of heaven. Moses had laboured under the illusion that God would release Israel from Pharaoh's bondage by his hands and wrongfully supposed that his brethren would have understood that. On the contrary, they understood not. Moses anticipated his people's release forty years before the scheduled timetable. Not until forty years later did God appear to him in the burning but unconsumed bush at Sinai. His recorded words to

Moses were, "I am come down to deliver them." He had made the journey from Heaven to Egypt for that very purpose, "and now come, I will send thee into Egypt to deliver them, by the hand of the angel who appeared to him in the bush" (Acts 7:34–5). Stephen said, "but Solomon built Him an house", which was a veritable stately edifice, and described as "exceeding magnifical, of fame" (1 Chron.22:5). Stephen, however, continued his inspired discourse with an astounding reminder, "Howbeit, the Most High dwelleth not in temples made with hands, as saith the prophet, Heaven is My throne, and earth is My footstool: what house will ye build Me? ... Hath not My hands made all these things?" (Acts 7:47–50). David got it right when in one of the psalms of degrees, he firmly stated, "Except the Lord build the house, they labour in vain that build it" (Psalm 127:1). In short, unless the Lord plans, provides and inspires its erection, it will fall down.

From which we may deduce that the 276 persons on board, making a sum total of 552 hands with their concerted efforts, failed to bring the ship to land, or subdue the fury of the tempest. Contrariwise, "When Christ by Himself had purged our sins, sat down on the right hand of the majesty on high" (Heb.1:3), and so it follows, that by this introduction to the epistle, the theme that threads its way throughout the range of the epistle, and with seeming impatience asks the question, "How shall we escape if we neglect so great salvation?" (Heb.2:3). When the end of the voyage is arrived at safely, it will be because "The holiest has been entered by the blood of Christ by a new and living way, which He hath consecrated for us, through the veil, that is to say His flesh; and having a High Priest over the House of God, let us draw near with a true heart, in full assurance of faith, having our hearts sprinkled from an evil conscience and our bodies washed with pure water" (Heb.10:19–22).

God ordered that circumcision should be the seal which distinguished the people of God from the children of this world. It was the sign of the special relationship between God and the family of Abraham, called the 'Household of Faith'. All born in his house or bought with money were charged to be circumcised in the flesh of their foreskin (Gen.17:12–13). Anyone ignoring this ritual and who was not circumcised would be cut off from the people of God (Gen.17:12–13). Those who submitted were regarded by God as being related to God with all the obligations of two parties bound together in covenant. Israel's peculiar relationship with God was therefore called a covenant relationship or agreement. Moses was immediately recognised as being a Hebrew child by the mark of circumcision. Non-Jews were known as Gentiles, and physically the seal of circumcision was the one distinguishing feature, which also was meant to distinguish them from all the uncircumcised as a holy nation. A title given by Israel to the Philistines was that of uncircumcised, and was a title of odium. It meant such a one was unclean and not separated to God. Even the removal of the skin by a physical operation was an operation that obviated physical filthiness, which is an emblem of the carnal or Adamite life of the natural man, whose significance is given a new and spiritual meaning in the New Covenant introduced by Christ in the Upper Room. His immemorial words are "This is the blood of the New Covenant", based not on the bloodletting caused by a physical operation, but the blood of Christ freely shed to bring Jews – circumcised bodily and performed by human hands; and Gentiles – having no bodily mutilation, together into a new spiritual relationship with God, in which all the blessings under the Old Covenant are transmuted into eternal blessings and a more intimate relationship as sons of God, with a heavenly and eternal inheritance, of which the moral is that the physical operation is no longer valid, and has no virtue instinct in it. What was physical has now become spiritual; that which was outward has been replaced by that which is inward; fleshly circumcision has given way to spiritual circumcision. Paul sums it up concisely at the close of the second chapter of Romans: "For He is not a Jew which is one outwardly; neither is that circumcision, which is outward in the flesh: but he is a Jew, which is one inwardly: and circumcision is that of the heart, in the spirit, and not in the letter; whose praise is not of men, but of God" (Rom.2:28–9).

Jewish circumcision in the New Testament setting is spoken of as being made by hands, and now represents all outward religion performed by human endeavour and carnal energy. Such was Paul's religion before his spiritual conversion or New Birth. Gentiles were called uncircumcision, by that which is called the circumcision, in the flesh made by hands (Ephes.2:11). Writing to the Colossians, the apostle hallmarking their privileges as believers declared, "And ye are complete in Christ, which is the head of all principality and power: in whom ye also are circumcised with the circumcision made without hands, in putting off the body of the sins of the flesh, by the circumcision of Christ" (Col.2:10–11). Paul wrote to the Philippians to "beware of the concision – a derisory term implying the cutting off of a piece of skin" (John Wesley). "For we are the circumcision who worship God in Spirit" (Phil.3:2–3), not with barely outward worship, but with the spiritual worship of inward holiness "and glory in Christ Jesus" as the only cause of all our blessings.

In, therefore, the voyage of life, everything superfluous, all man-inspired religion, such as outward zeal for a cause or a church or a body of rules, or a conformity to ritualism or ceremony, idealism or humanism, all the work of men's hands, all comprising so much ballast, need to be parted with. Paul summed all these things up under the expression "confidence in the flesh" (Phil.3:3–4). All are to be cast away, to ensure that we ourselves shall not be castaways.

* * * * * * * * * * * * * * * * * * * *

SERMON 9

THE ECLIPSE OF HOPE AND THE DAWN OF DELIVERANCE

Acts 27:20: *And when neither sun nor stars appeared in many days, and no small tempest lay on us, all hope that we should be saved was then taken away.*

Hope has been defined as the anticipation of future good, which has therefore a benign influence on the present. Conversely "deferred hope" – otherwise disappointment – "maketh the heart sick" (Prov.13:12), for disappointment robs the present of happiness, as for example, a person on holiday who receives news of a failed examination loses all interest in pleasure for the remainder of the holiday. Any life that has lost all hope is one of despair. Strenuous but futile exertion to ride out the storm had reduced the ship's crew and company to a state of despair. The rosy hopes they had entertained on sailing away from the port of Fair Havens were sorely blighted.

Moreover, the unabated intensity and drawn-out nature of the storm was further aggravated by the absence of sun and stars, enshrouding them in a perpetual gloom which corresponded with the despair of their spirits.

To be without sun spelled the absence of light and heat and power, and is applicable spiritually to all who are devoid of the Sun of Righteousness, who incorporates these factors. Malachi declared, "But to you who fear My name shall the Sun of Righteousness arise with healing in His wings or rays" (Mal.4:3). It is impossible to experience salvation without "truth in the inward parts" (Psalm 51:6), apart from which "the spirit is in darkness, blinded by the god of this world" (2 Cor.4:3–4) as realistically as darkness was upon the face of the deep, until the LORD commanded the light to shine out of darkness" (Gen.1:2–3). All unbelievers have this in common: they have been blinded by Satan and remain so until Christ the Sun of Righteousness arises within them to diffuse the rays of divine truth into their minds. And an awareness of this is essential before real hope can break upon the individual soul. Paradoxically, it is at the point of despair of achieving salvation, which is the harbinger of deliverance. Seekers after God and salvation must first be brought to the end of themselves before they begin to experience their personal reality. Psalm 107:20–30 sets forth the case admirably. Mariners aboard a storm-tossed ship are depicted as by turns tossed up to the heavens and plunged into the depths, and described as being at their wits' end, whose souls are melted because of trouble. At their wits' end has been literally rendered, "All their nautical skill is exhausted, which has bereft them of hope. In desperation they turn to praying, when they cry unto the LORD in their trouble and He bringeth them out of their distresses… So He bringeth them to their desired haven".

Abraham's long-cherished hope of a son by Sarah and all other natural means dried up at ninety-nine years of age, by which age his body was dead, meaning that he was then incapable of reproduction. Far from feeling despondent, "Against hope he believed in hope". Two insurmountable barriers were "the deadness of Sarah's womb" and "the deadness of his own body" (Rom.4:18–19). Where death reigns, hope has died. A striking comment on this is provided in Romans 7 with the agonised cry of a man hemmed in by death, or figuratively, with a corpse strapped to his body, and poignantly expressed, "O wretched man that I am! Who shall deliver me from the body of this death or dead body?" (Rom.7:24). By the body of death Paul meant this body of sin leading to death. In vain had he wriggled and squirmed to dislodge it, which was clinging to his soul like a tight-fitting garment to his body, or like the lamprey fish to a salmon, to which it attached itself with vice-like jaws, and was sucking its life force. With all hope gone Paul turned to the LORD, who immediately emancipated him, so that his cry of agony was turned to a paean of praise: "I thank God through Jesus Christ our LORD" (Rom.7:25).

Sisera's mother waited impatiently for the return of her long-overdue son from the battle. She soliloquised, and said, "He is detained dividing the spoil, of which there would be much, but it was a vain hope." Sisera was dead with a tent pin through his head: he would never return (Judges 5:24–31).

Before anyone can be saved they must be brought to the end of themselves. Only then will "The Sun of Righteousness arise with healing in His rays" (Mal.4:2). This same principle must be implemented in that which applies to "the rest of God" as says the Scripture: "There remaineth therefore a rest to the people of God. For he that is entered into His rest, he also hath ceased from his own works, as God *did* from His" (Heb.4:9–10). After forty years of wandering in the desert, Joshua brought the people of God into Canaan and exterminated the seven Canaanitish ethnic groups of aborigines; the land rested from war. Likewise, by faith the people of God in Christ rest from their wanderings of unbelief and their long struggles against "fleshly lusts which war against the soul" (1 Peter 2:11). This successful sequel of the rest of God is achieved not by striving but by trusting: not by struggling but by surrendering.

The absence of the sun implies a want of warmth or heat. A heart devoid of the warmth of the love of God is in a miserable state and is out of fellowship with the risen LORD. None would disagree that the natural sun is the source of heat. Likewise the heart that is familiar with the risen Saviour is filled with the abundance of consolations in Christ and enjoys much of the comfort and warmth of the love of God (Phil.2:1). Psalm 19 in reference to the sun adopts the simile of a bridegroom emerging from his bedchamber rejoicing and bounding across the heavenly circuit as a strong man running a race. His circuit is cited as from the end of heaven and reaches to the ends of it, declaring, "And there is nothing hid from the heat thereof" (Psalm 19:4–6). Everything on which it shines feels its warm glow. When the love of Christ is absent from the heart, salvation is mere wishful thinking. For the want of it the apostle invokes a devastating imprecation, saying, "If any man love not our LORD Jesus Christ, let him be Anathema Maranatha, that is accursed" (1 Cor.16:22).

From the standpoint of power, the sun is the greatest in the universe. Through its agency God causeth vapours to ascend from the ends of the earth. Billions of tons of water are airlifted daily by constant evaporation. The ratio of evaporation is equivalent to the tonnage of water poured into the sea every day by the numerous rivers of the world. So great is the volume and force of the waters of the mighty Amazon that fresh water is found 500 miles out at sea. Someone has estimated scientifically that to evaporate by thermal means all the waters airlifted yearly would require an amount of coal that could be found filling a half-dozen worlds such as ours. Of all power, Christ's Gospel is the greatest demonstrator. Its peculiar classification is that "it is the power of God unto salvation to everyone who believes". No other energy or agency, apart from the Gospel of Christ, can save a man from his sins, transform his life from a sinner to a saint and eventually get him into heaven, having escaped the damnation of hell. In the current story of the shipwreck, when they lost the sun they lost all hope of salvation. However, "those upon whom Christ the Sun of Righteousness arises have spiritual health and strength, light and salvation, delight and joy, safety and security" (John Wesley).

One of the most charming episodes with which the epic of the resurrection sparkles is the narration of Christ's encounter with Cleopas and his partner on the sixty-furlong stretch of road between Jerusalem and Emmaus. They were sad because they had lost the sun. For three days they had lost all trace of Him; He had been effectually blotted out, leaving their minds dark and perplexed. After a marathon exposition of the Scriptures by the LORD they arrived on their doorstep, at sunset. During the journey Christ had been pouring light on the pages of Holy Writ and their numerous references to Himself, which was joined with a warmth in their own hearts.

Hardly had they sat down to enjoy a late meal, when as He gave thanks and blessed the bread, His identity was disclosed. Outside the sun was setting inside Christ the Sun of Righteousness, with a blaze of glory made His presence known. They had, in fact, felt this on their journey home which they had expressed in those well-known timeless words: "Did not our heart burn within us?" etc (Luke 24:32). Before His vanishing out of their sight, their darkness was passed: they had received the light of His truth, the warmth of His love, and the energy of his power. Galvanised by the latter, in spite of the lateness of the hour they rose up without delay, and returned to Jerusalem to report the most wonderful news the world would ever hear. All their weariness was forgotten; their hunger was forgotten; the dangers of the road late at night were forgotten. Christ had been made known to them (Luke 24:30–5).

Yet another aggravation of the ship's plight was the absence of the stars. Safe sailing at night-time was only possible when the skies were cloudless and disclosed the thousands of stars that studded the heavens that could be seen with the naked eye, and, because of their fixed positions relative to each other, constituted the mariner's chart and compass. Those were the days before the invention of the binnacle which contained the compass found in all modern ships, and which homes onto the North Star of the Northern Hemisphere – the main direction pointer.

God's witnesses are sometimes likened to stars, through whose ministries men and women are directed to Christ and eventually to heaven. In being thus directed they escape the danger of the loss of their souls, and eternal disaster. They themselves are guided by the unerring truth, and are said "to shine as lights in the world" – designated "a crooked and perverse generation" (Phil.2:15).

Hearing a trumpet voice behind him, John turned round and descried a circle of seven golden candlesticks, in the centre of which was One like the Son of Man, holding seven stars in His right hand, and was informed that they were the angels or messengers, alias pastors of the seven churches in Asia. Theirs was the responsibility of preaching the Word concerning which their instructions were to "be instant in season, out of season; reprove, rebuke, exhort with all longsuffering and doctrine" (2 Tim.4:2). Likewise they were admonished "to be examples of the believers, in word, in conversation, in charity, in spirit, in faith, in purity" (1 Tim.12:4). So transparent and radiant with light were they charged to become, that believers and unbelievers could take their cue from them and not miss the road that leads to heaven.

A story related in the earlier chapters of the Acts is of Philip the evangelist, who had been the mainspring of a sweeping revival in Samaria, but his ministry there was abruptly brought to a close, and a new directive delivered by the angel of the LORD required him to proceed south to the desert of Gaza. Upon his arrival he saw the person he was to make contact with who was the treasurer of Candace the Ethiopian monarch. The man was journeying leisurely in his chariot on his way back from Jerusalem. He was deeply engrossed in reading aloud from the book of Isaiah. The Spirit spoke to Philip and told him to go and speak with this Ethopian eunuch. Philip ran alongside the chariot and asked the eunuch if he understood the passage that he was reading and the eunuch's answer revealed the darkness of his mind, but of his willingness to learn: "How can I except some man should guide me?" Philip, upon the treasurer's invitation, sat with him in his chariot and picked up the threads of the scripture he was reading, and preached unto him Jesus from the excerpt: "He was led as a lamb to the slaughter, and as a sheep before her shearers is dumb so He opened not his mouth" (Acts 8:32–5). So quickly did the eunuch grasp the truth of Christ and His salvation that he willingly submitted himself to baptism at a wayside pool (Acts 8:38–9). His mission completed in guiding the Ethiopian to Christ, Philip was supernaturally transported by the Spirit – airlifted probably – to Azotus (Acts 8:39).

The absence of stars betokens the want of guidance by the Spirit of God. Almost the last thing that Christ promised the disciples was of "sending them another Comforter", who would take His place. His prime errand of the Spirit of God would be to guide them into all truth. Christ expanded on the role of the Spirit of God saying, "He will not speak of Himself... He shall glorify Me: for He shall receive of Mine, and shall shew it unto you" (John 16:13–14). None but those "who are led by the Spirit of God are the sons of God" (Rom.8:14).

A fascinating incident in the story of Christ's advent is the part played by the wise men from the east. They saw Christ's star in the east and journeyed hundreds of miles to Judæa to pay homage to the King of the Jews, as betokened by the star. Expecting to hear of His birth at Jerusalem, they were nonplussed to learn that the people there had no knowledge of the event. All the Jewish theologians could say was that Christ's birth would be at Bethlehem. Only after they rerouted to Bethlehem did the star they had seen two years before reappear, and went before them and came and stood over where the young child was. Seeing the star again caused them to rejoice with exceedingly great joy, which gave place to wonder when "they entered the house and saw the young child with Mary His mother". Their joy was superseded by something that far transcended it. "They fell down and worshipped Him" (Matt.2:9–11). God's Spirit always leads to God's Son, in whom alone is salvation. He is Christ's star. With no star to give them any clue of their whereabouts the shipmen were left in a perilous position; disaster seemed inevitable.

God's promises in the hemisphere of Holy Writ are like stars of varying magnitudes. Peter writes about them as "exceeding great and precious promises, by which they become partakers of the divine nature, having escaped the corruption which is in the world through lust" (2 Peter 1:4). Paul, likewise, extols the promises in which God hath said, "I will dwell in them and walk in them ... I will be a Father unto you, and ye shall be My sons and daughters, saith the LORD Almighty" (2 Cor.6:16–18). God's promises reflect the whole of salvation and were designed to be possessed and not simply admired. Where, however, there is no star, there is no promise, and a non-existent promise infers "all hope that we shall be saved is taken away" (verse 26).

The widow woman of Syro-Phenicia (Canaan) had a massive family problem, which impelled her to seek the LORD, having personally witnessed His miracles of healing on the borders of Tyre and Sidon (Matt.15:21). She had been convinced her only hope was in Christ; hence the quest. Her daughter was grievously vexed with a devil, but her request was double-barrelled: she appealed for mercy for herself: "Have mercy on me", and "grant deliverance to my daughter". She was mentally distraught; her daughter was physically abused. Christ's response to the woman's moving entreaty was negative: "But He answered her not a word". Her persistence took her to His disciples, but their utter bankruptcy of any ability to help was reflected in their embarrass-ment and an appeal to Christ to send her away by acceding to her request. To that request, Christ's response was a technical one: "I am not sent but to the lost sheep of the House of Israel", which could well be construed as meaning "My mission is to Israel and not to the Gentiles; I have no promise for them". Still undeterred, she fell down and worshipped Him, with a pathetic appeal, "LORD help me". Her desperation is to be noted in the brevity of her prayer. Long rambling prayers usually indicate a lack of feeling and intensity, if not sincerity. Peter's succinct cry, as he began to sink, was, "LORD save me". In times of crisis there is no time for protracted praying. Christ's reply to her poignant last-ditch effort to the untuned ear, was nothing if not brutal: "It is not right to take the children's bread and cast it to the dogs" at which point the LORD was completely disarmed by the humility of her reply, which was one of thorough agreement with His devaluation of Gentile stock, when she and her Gentile fraternity were classified with the dogs. Even Christ's disciples must have been embarrassed by the forthrightness of their Master's castigation. Perhaps silently they soliloquised, "He has gone too far!" As if by divine inspiration she said, doubtless in all humility, "Truth LORD, yet the dogs eat of the crumbs which fall from their master's table". Her sheer trust had broken through the darkness, and her doomed daughter was delivered (Matt.15:22–8).

Isaiah the prophet has the complete answer to persistent and unrelieved darkness, for such are those who lack the assurance of salvation. His words are "Who is he among you that feareth the LORD, that obeyeth the voice of His servant, that walketh in darkness, and hath no light? Neither sun nor stars: Let him trust in the name of the LORD, and stay upon his God" (Isaiah 50:10).

* * * * * * * * * * * * * * * * * * * *

SERMON 10

GOOD NEWS FOR A REBELLIOUS COMPANY

Acts 27:21–22: *But after long abstinence Paul stood forth in the midst of them, and said, Sirs, ye should have hearkened unto me, and not have loosed from Crete, and to have gained this harm and loss. And now I exhort you to be of good cheer: for there shall be no loss of any man's life among you, but of the ship.*

Rebellion against God is endemic in the human race. For that reason humans are classified by God as children of disobedience. Disobedience is woven into the warp and woof of their nature. "Like father, like son" is true of Adam's descendants. Truly "they are chips off the old block". Adam began the fashion, and, of all places, in the Garden of Delights, otherwise the Garden of Eden, and because they are "Children of Disobedience", they have become "Children of wrath by nature" (Ephes.2:2–3).

The Gospel call is a call to obedience: rebellion is in effect saying "No" to God and "Yes" to one's self. All the books of the prophets register God's protests against human waywardness, which is fully borne out by a trail of blood of dead prophets, from "Abel to Zechariah who perished – murdered – between the Temple and the Altar" (Matt.23:25).

Paul's admonition had been treated with disdain. He had given the ship's officers sound advice that was combined with a warning, which is often the case with people, when the warning would deny them the luxury of pleasing themselves. Every cigarette packet carries a government warning, but millions of people disparage it and carry on smoking. In the midst of Eden's sylvan beauty was a deadly poisonous tree, and the warning notice said so: death is immediate to all who eat of this fruit, signed by the highest authority, the proprietor of the Garden and the God of Heaven. Of all the trees in the Garden it was the most flamboyant and called the "Tree of the Knowledge of Good and Evil" (Gen 3:17). Psalm 107:10–14 draws attention to men who were at death's door, bound with affliction and iron because they rebelled against the words of God and contemned the counsel of the Most High. Audaciously, they despised it. Daniel's severe reprimand to Belshazzar was set against his father Nebuchadnezzar's humility, after his seven years' degradation, of being reduced to the level of an ox grazing in the meadow, from which he had learned nothing. Daringly he toasted his gods of gold and silver, and brass and stone with the sacred vessels of the Temple in Jerusalem that had been sacked by the Babylonians seventy years before. Nebuchadnezzar had admitted his folly and repented. Belshazzar spoke not one word of regret or remorse though the hand of the divine messenger wrote his judgement on the wall of his banqueting chamber before a thousand guests. That night he was slain by the Persian soldiers at the foot of his own throne (Daniel 5:25–31).

Disobedience always occasions loss. The ship's officers and the Centurion were told they would lose the ship and its cargo. In that era there were no Lloyd's shipping underwriters; a loss at sea was a total loss. Adam's disobedience cost him God's presence and fellowship; a forfeiture of the divine image. He became like a marred earthen vessel. His delegated power over the creature had been cast to the four winds and never regained, but was super-seded by the beast's fear of him. And, most disastrously of all, he lost heaven and eternal life. And the same holds good to this present day: "The wages of sin is death" (Rom.6:23).

The heinousness of their rebellion lay in honouring the ship-owner more than Paul the servant of God. By a similar parity Adam in his reckless disobedience had honoured the god of this world – having hijacked it – more than God its rightful owner and maker. He had pitted the world's wisdom, which is at best folly, against the infallible and unsearchable wisdom of God. "O the depth of the riches of the wisdom of God. How unsearchable are His judgements and His ways past finding out" (Rom.11:33).

An ordeal of such terrifying magnitude, in which "they were exceedingly tossed with a tempest", resulted from their listening to the wrong voice, as explained by the prophet Isaiah. Speaking for the LORD, he lamented, "O that thou hadst hearkened unto My commandments, then hadst thy peace been as a river!" which glides along peacefully and noiselessly, and quite unlike the roaring winds and raging waves of their present ordeal (Isaiah 48:18). In heaven, where God is always obeyed, we are reminded "there will be no more sea" (Rev.21:1), but there is "a pure river of water of life proceeding out of the throne of God and of the Lamb" (Rev.22:1). It is a picture of the River of God or of "The Holy Ghost, given to those who obey God" (Acts 5:32).

Paul's confrontation with the ship's complement is taken notice of: "He stood forth in the midst". He would have everyone's attention: he stood out by standing forth. No one has any right to assume a commanding stance who has not first of all concealed himself. Elijah obeyed God when told to hide himself, and so conscientious was he in secreting himself, that although King Ahab went through the land and neighbouring countries for three and a half years with a toothcomb, he found not a single hair. Having had a second order to show himself to Ahab and 450 prophets of Baal and all Israel represented at Carmel, he stood out conspicuously (I Kings 18:20–1).

It is said that it was after long abstinence that Paul emerged from a place of privacy, either in the well or hold of the ship. Prayer and fasting had engaged him for fourteen days. Later in the story Paul reminded all on board that they had taken nothing for that same period, but for a radically different reason from his: the fear of approaching death had robbed them of their appetites. But Paul had no such terror. If everyone else perished God had told him "he must appear before Cæsar". His reason for refusing food was that he would by prayer and fasting prevail with God and secure the lives of all on board. Christ's remedy for the deliverance of distressed souls is the infallible one: "When ye pray, enter into your closet and pray to your Father who is in secret, and your Father who seeth in secret, will reward you openly" (Matt.6:6). Mark how God rewarded Elijah: a whole nation publicly confessed Jehovah's supremacy with a vociferous outburst, "The Lord He is the God; The Lord He is the God" (1 Kings 18:39).

Paul first of all reminded them of their own folly, and of the accuracy of his own earlier warning. He had something more to tell them, which was guaranteed to buoy up their spirits, as good news always does in a situation of despair. He exhorted them "to be of good cheer", which, in the absence of all hope was all the more welcome. As Paul had been in Asia, "They were pressed out of measure beyond strength and despaired even of life" (2 Cor.1:8). Christ's message is called 'the Gospel', literally God's spell or God's story, which equates to good news, which in our world is a rare thing and a novelty indeed, for bad news is the norm. Scan the front page of the popular press and little of an elevating or encouraging vein is found thereon; much if not most of the copy has to do with trouble of a varying sort: disasters, crises, crime, murder, scandal and economic instability.

Paul's message of "Good Cheer" was expressed by a dying Christian tar. When asked by a fellow sailor, in nautical language, "What cheer?" he replied, "Good cheer, land in sight." When the fellow sailor visited him the following day and asked the same question he received the answer as before: "Good cheer, rounded the cape, pilot aboard". His answer to the same question on the third day was the same but spoken in a weaker voice, "Good cheer, in port, dropped anchor, safe home."

The apostle's message of good cheer was in startling contrast to the character of his audience, who to a man were a rebellious company. Of Christ it is written, "When He ascended up on high,

He led captivity captive, He gave gifts to men and for the rebel-lious also" (Psalm 68:18; Ephes.4:8).

Christ's cross and sufferings and victorious emergence from hell and entry into heaven resembled the triumphal procession of a returning victorious Roman army, with the conquered command-ers chained to their chariots, and of the donatives or gifts thrown to the admiring and cheering spectators.

They had been expecting death, and therefore the news of life was all the more welcome. No better news could have been conveyed to them. A man in the death cell hears the bolts of his cell door being drawn, to reveal the governor of the prison framed in the doorway, holding an official looking document in his hand, and who reads it to him: his sentence has been commuted to life imprisonment. How relieved would he be! How much more so if the declaration said that his death sentence had been completely abrogated, without conditions, then the truth of the proverb would be demonstrated: "The heart knoweth its own bitterness, and a stranger doth not intermeddle with his joy" (Prov.14:10) as with the rebel soldier who had repeatedly flouted his commanding officer's orders and had finally deserted from his colours, but was eventually caught and court-martialed, whereupon the death sentence was pronounced against him. The soldier heard the sentence without showing any emotion. He was taken back to his cell to await the day of execution. At the appointed day and hour, the commanding officer appeared to apprise him of the time of execution, and cited all the things he had been guilty of, for which he had shown no remorse. In spite of this the General declared, "I have decided to waive the death penalty. You are a forgiven and free man." To the army chief's astonishment, the rebel before him, who had never given any hint of feeling or display of remorse, broke down like a child. The gift of life and the mercy of the General prevailed where threat and punishment had left him unmoved. Of the same tenor is the message of good cheer of Christ and the Gospel. Of straying sheep Christ the good shepherd said, "I am come that they might have life, and that they might have *it* more abundantly" (John 10:10) and later added, "I give unto them eternal life" (John 10:20).

What small fry is the news of inheriting a fortune compared with that of being made the recipient of eternal life. Mark the reaction of Zacchaeus to Christ's intention to spend that day at his house, and a little later that salvation had come to his house. An integral part of salvation is the idea of deliverance from death and the enjoyment of eternal life. John Wesley remarked, "How sweet is the thought of eternal life to those who are Christ's sheep!" Jeremiah made clear what life's priority is, saying, "Let not the wise man glory in his wisdom, nor the strong man in his strength, nor the rich man in his riches: But let him that glorieth glory in this, that he understandeth and knoweth Me" (Jer.9:23–4).

When Elijah raised the dead son of the woman of Zarephath to life, he said, "See thy son liveth". The woman's awestruck response was, "Now, by this I know that thou art a man of God, and that the Word of the LORD in thy mouth is truth" (1 Kings 17:23–4). Mephibosheth's apprehension must have been greater than his surprise when the messenger from King David stood outside his door in Lo-debar, with an urgent message for him to return with him to Jerusalem; so much so that upon his arrival, he fell on his face before David, with fear plainly registered in his eyes, knowing nothing of the covenant of perpetual friendship between David and Jonathan his father, and their families (1 Sam.23:28; 1 Sam.20:16–17) for there was no survivor or legal heir of Saul and his family, apart from Jonathan Sanl's young son. A fact of history is that survivors of a past dynasty can become dangerous rivals, as were the Jacobite pretenders thorns in the side of William and Mary of Orange. He called himself a dead dog, but David's words "Fear not for I will assuredly show thee kindness" – literally the kindness of God – "for Jonathan thy father's sake" (2 Sam.9:7) were reassuring.

Paul expressly said, "There shall be no loss of any man's life among you but of the ship". As the captain was the ringleader of the rebellion he would be made to smart. His decision to weigh anchor and set sail had endangered the lives of all for the sake of gain. His loss of the grain ship, which was of heavy tonnage, for no small ship could have accommodated 276 personnel and a large cargo of grain, would most probably have spelled ruin for him. Learning by experience is always a costly folly.

Superficially there would seem to be a contradiction in the episode. Paul had warned the captain and shipowner, with Julian, that to leave their safe harbour would be to pursue an elusive will-o'-the-wisp. He had emphasised that it would be a costly adventure with "much damage to the cargo and ship but more seriously of their lives" (verse 10). His strong implication more than suggested that there would be loss of some, if not all, of their lives. However, the worst was not realised. Paul set himself to pray protractedly and intensively for the salvation of all on board, and so effectual were his prayers that a wholesale disaster was staved off, and there were no human casualties, as indeed was the case with the doomed city of Nineveh. Jonah's message was neither a threat nor a warning. No quarter would be given. His denunciation was unequivocal: "Yet forty days and Nineveh shall be destroyed". There is only one explanation that it was not destroyed. Jonah had left no loophole in his message; no star of promise of hope appeared in their midnight sky of impending disaster. On a vague "Who can tell whether God will turn and repent and turn away from His fierce anger, that we perish not?", king and people donned sackcloth and turned from their wicked ways, for coupled with their deep and sincere humiliation was the fact – which weighed heavily with a just God and a holy – of "one hundred and twenty thousand innocent children and a huge herd of dumb beasts" (Jonah 4:11). Because "they turned from their evil way, God repented of the evil He said He would do, and He did it not" (Jonah 3:10).

James summed the matter up in the latter part of the final

chapter of his epistle, where prayer is mentioned seven times. In one succinct comprehensive statement he dogmatically declared, "The effectual fervent prayer of a righteous man availed much" (James 5:16). Paul proved it on the battered grain ship of Alexandria, in an unremitting tempest.

* * * * * * * * * * * * * * * * * * * *

SERMON 11

PAUL THE MAN AND SERVANT OF GOD

Acts 27:23–4: *For there stood by me this night the angel of God, whose I am, and whom I serve, Saying, Fear not, Paul; thou must be brought before Cæsar: and, lo, God hath given thee all them that sail with thee.*

It was essential that those on board, especially the centurion and the ship's captain and owner, be made aware of the status of the illustrious prisoner, whose advice they had ignored, as though he were a bigoted know-all. Before the journey was over they would be convinced the boot was on the other foot, and that *they*, and not Paul, were the ignoramuses. If they would be saved from their folly of death, they were being advised to take Paul seriously, and his message with the respect it demanded, as coming from God.

Luke had counted 276 people on board: Paul counted 277. No one but Paul saw the angel or heavenly messenger, or heard him deliver the message, although he stood by the apostle, whose business it was to receive heavenly news and pass it on to those concerned. The angel of God's mission was to one person only, namely Paul the man of God.

Paul was such because he had been born of God, or from above. He was a man of another world, and of another nature. He corrected Claudius Lysias, who mistook him for an Egyptian, by telling him he was a Jew of Tarsus, a citizen of no mean city, yet, in a far greater sense, that he was a citizen of the heavenly Jerusalem. But his being a freeborn Roman citizen was infinitely below the dignity of being born of "Jerusalem which is above, which is free, that is the mother of us all" who believe in Christ (Gal.4:26). In an astonishing figure of speech Paul was waited upon by God from his birth, when as in the role of a midwife He separated him from his mother's womb and revealed His Son in him (Gal.1:15–16).

Furthermore, his high station was to be deduced from God's complete involvement in Paul's affairs. After being separated – that is, set apart for special service – he had been called by His grace. Although designated from birth, the actual call did not come until years later when Paul was en route to Damascus with murder in his heart which was spoken of as "breathing out threatenings and slaughter" (Acts 9:1), and he was called literally by name, "Saul, Saul" (Acts 9:4). From that moment he was appraised of the lofty dignity of his calling, as stated in some of his letters, "called to be an apostle" (Rom.1:1, 1 Cor.1:1). Ananias was sent to him three days later to inform him that "the God of their fathers had called him to be a witness to all men" and thereby substantiated Christ's words, "I have appeared unto thee to make thee a minister, and a witness … delivering thee from the Gentiles, to whom now I send thee" (Acts 26:16 –17).

As God owned Job before Satan with the pointed question, "Hast thou considered My servant Job?" (Job 1:3), which words were spoken to Satan, whose knowledge of men's actions – but not their thoughts – was second to none, so four times in speaking to Eliphaz, Job's chief critic, rebuking him from his errors of judgement against him, called him "My servant Job" (Job 42:7–8). One of the signal methods of God to demonstrate the proprietorship of His own, is that of answering their prayers. Of Job He said to Eliphaz and his friends, "For I will accept him" (Job 42:8), and charged them to seek his good offices. Indeed, those whom God owns are His favourites. God accounted Ananias's reluctance to proceed to Straight Street in Damascus and minister to the distressed Saul, by an unambiguous declaration, "Go thy way, he is a chosen vessel unto Me" (Acts 9:15).

Paul was honoured by God more than any person of his day. On board that boat that was being battered with mountainous waves and cyclonic winds, he entertained a visitor from heaven. Under any other circumstances, Paul's testimony of an angelic messenger would have met with derision, and been tantamount to casting pearls before swine. Virtually every person on board was devoid of the fear of God, as well as being coarse and godless. Danger, however, subdues the worst characters, and it must always be true that "a drowning man will clutch at any straw". One is singularly struck by the implications of Paul's naïve statement. Everyone on board was lost upon the high seas that leave no footprints, and was without the slightest notion of their latitude and longitude. When Paul discoursed to the learned Athenian pundits and the judiciary on Mars Hill, in a city whose reputation was that it was easier to find a god in Athens than a man, in spite of which the apostle reminded the Greek intelligentsia of their ignorance of God the creator of the world, yet, if they would seek Him they would find Him, for "He is not far from every one of us" (Acts 17:27). God was lost to them, as was their geographical location, but the angel from His immediate presence needed neither sun nor stars nor compass to find them.

Job once complained that he had lost God, in such words as "Behold, I go forward, but He is not there; and backward, but I cannot perceive Him; on the left hand, where He doth work, but I cannot behold Him: He hideth Himself on the right hand, that I cannot see Him: but He knoweth the way that I take" (Job 23:8–10). In effect Job said, "I don't know where God is [though He was with him all the time] but He knows where I am", and not until the end of the discourse, which was summed up by the ever present omnipotent God, did Job arrive at a clear revelation of Him. Job's humble and frank admission was, "I have heard of Thee by the hearing of the ear: but now mine eye seeth Thee" (Job 42:5). While God is lost to the majority of men, men are never lost to Him; never are they beyond the range of His vision or the reach of His arm. Christ saw Nathaniel under the fig tree and could tell him the matter he was thinking about (John 1:47–8). Zacchæus thought himself hidden amongst the umbrageous foliage of the sycamore tree, but must have been delightfully astonished when called by name and called by Christ to entertain Him in his home (Luke 19:6).

John Newton, who was later to become one of London's most powerful preachers and a celebrated hymn composer, was in his younger years a virtual prisoner of an unscrupulous woman on the west coast of Africa. His sole possession was a shirt and a pair of trousers. Work had been consigned to him on a barren and uninhabited part of the coast. Any possibility of escape was almost nil. His chances of seeing Britain again were remote. It was a part of the coast where few ships passed. One day, he espied one in the distance. It occurred to him that he might attract its attention. Lighting a fire, he endeavoured to send a smoke signal, praying that someone might see it and raise the alarm. To his dismay, the ship continued on course, seemingly unaware of his distress signal. Just when he had given up hope the ship suddenly changed course, and within a while a boat was launched, heading in his direction. Great was the surprise of the captain and crew upon finding an unkempt and ragged Englishman on that lonely stretch of coast. Not only was John Newton rescued from a wretched and degrading future, but he soon became set on course for heaven. God knew where he was, and providentially sent a ship – a rare occurrence – in his direction. Had he only ever written the hymn 'Amazing Grace' with the line, "I once was lost but now am found" he would have bequeathed a priceless boon to a lost society.

The angel who stood by Paul – perhaps Gabriel – was sent to reassure him and, through him, everyone on board, that everything was well in hand. There would be no fatalities. Paul's petition had been granted for the safety of the 275 others. Not a single one would be absent at the muster of the survivors on the shore of Melita. Every genuine answer to prayer is a sure mark of God's favour, as with Noah, Daniel and Job (Ezek.14:14–20), who were given all that sailed with them. Paul had asked for all, even for the obstreperous captain and owner; and God gave him all.

Moses prayed for his criticising and jealous sister Miriam – jealous of a coloured sister-in-law – and God removed the disfigurement and humiliating stigma of leprosy from her. God, thus, vindicated His servant Moses, and paid him the tribute of being the most faithful servant in His house, and asked, "Wherefore, then, were ye not afraid to speak against My servant Moses?" (Numbers 12:8). Miriam was put out of the camp for seven days, to bring home to her the wickedness of her criticism, and that others might fear. God defended the severity of His treatment with a strange observation, declaring, "Had her father spit in her face, such would have been her punishment". Much more, when God, by striking her with leprosy, spat, as it were, in her face for a much graver offence of slander against Moses and against his wife (Numbers 12:14–16).

God honoured Paul before the full complement of soldiers, seamen and prisoners. Julian's already high opinion would be further heightened. And the story has shades of the commander of the ship crossing the Atlantic, in which George Muller was a passenger who related the incident of a dramatic answer to prayer of God's servant. A dense fog caused the ship's speed to be reduced to dead slow. Muller told the commander that he was due to keep an appointment the following day in Montreal, and that he had never been late for one, and added, "I do not intend to be late for this one", to which the captain replied, "You can see the fog!" George Muller's rejoinder was, "My eyes are not on the fog, but on the God of the elements. Shall we go down into the state room and pray?" There and then this man of God prayed, and the captain, who was an avowed Christian, began to pray but was stopped by Muller, who said, "Don't pray: you don't believe. Beside, there is no need. God has answered prayer. Let us go on deck", and upon doing so observed there was not a wisp of the fog to be seen. That testimony was given not by Muller but by the captain to a passenger on his next voyage to North America. Truly, "They who go down to the sea in ships and do business in great waters, these see the works of the LORD and His wonders in the deep" (Psalm 107:23–4).

Paul's encounter with the messenger from God was a verification of an earlier assignment. This latter message ran, "Fear not, Paul; thou must be brought before Cæsar", and confirmed the previous one received in person from Christ while in custody in the castle barracks of the Roman legions at Jerusalem, who spoke words of goodwill and encouragement, saying, "Be of good cheer, Paul, for as thou hast testified of Me at Jerusalem so must thou also bear witness at Rome" (Acts 23:11). A subtle difference is to be noted in the prefatory phrases: Christ enjoined him "to be of good cheer" or joy, because of the harshness of the Jews towards him; the angel told him not to fear at the prospect of a confrontation with the ruthless despot Nero. Christ, who gave both Jezebels of the Old and New Testaments space to repent, would have Nero and his cohorts without excuse when that moment arrived; the apostle stood his ground as indomitably as Shammah who stood in the midst of a field of lentils, against a troop of Philistines, when the people fled; "and the LORD wrought a great victory" (2 Samuel 23:11–12). Of that encounter Paul said, "All men forsook me, but the LORD stood with me, and I was delivered out of the mouth of the lion" (2 Tim.4:16–17). Christ verily had a servant who would champion His cause before the religious hierarchy at Jerusalem, the hub of Judaism, and who was ready to take up the cudgels on His behalf before the pagan regime of the Roman Empire. It requires rare courage to discharge one's duty in such hostile company.

Furthermore, the imperativeness of the duty is greatly emphasised by repetition. Christ had said, "Thou *must* bear witness at Rome". The angel said, "Thou *must* be brought before Cæsar".

'Must' leaves no room for the leverage of self-pleasing, no more than Christ's stricture, "Marvel not that I say unto you, ye must be born again". In his vision of the descending New Jerusalem out of heaven from God, John noted twelve gates let into the four high walls that faced the four cardinal points. All the gates were of the same material; every several gate was of one pearl (Rev.21:12–21), which, of course, are formed within the bi-valves of the oyster, and caused by pain, the counterpart of which is the painful cross of suffering, on which "He bore our sins in His body on the tree, that we being dead to sins should live unto righteousness" (1 Peter 3:24). Christ's sufferings opened the gate which produced the Church of Christ. Paul stressed the truth, when confirming the young churches of Lystria, Iconium and Antioch that "we must through much tribulation enter into the kingdom of God" (Acts 14:21–22), first possibly alluding to Christ's tribulation or trouble, and second the tribulation of all who willingly espouse His cause and who take up His cross daily and follow Him.

Paul was proud to own himself a servant of God who owned him. Not only did he say, "Whose I am" but with equal pleasure, "Whom I serve". Among the wonders of King Solomon's court that indelibly impressed the Queen of Sheba, was "the sitting of his servants and their apparel or livery" (2 Kings 10:5).

Paul's claim to celestial service was twofold, which is more than hinted at in the command to Abraham to circumcise every male in his household, whether born in his house or bought with money (Gen 17:12–13). Like the Corinthians he had been bought from bondage to sin to that of a bond slave or servant of Christ. In strong language he reminded them, "that ye are not your own, for ye are bought with a price: therefore glorify God in your body and in your spirit which are God's" (1 Cor.6:19– 20). Christ displayed His hands and His feet to His terrified disciples in the upper room, but three days before, those same hands, in that same upper room, were unpierced. And to calm their troubled spirits, He invited them to "behold His hands and His feet" (Luke 24:39–40).

David's lament was echoed in Christ the Son of David's harrowing experience: "They pierced My hands and My feet" (Psalm 22:16), and were the all-sufficient proof of His resurrection and of the validity and sufficiency of man's redemption. Paul identified with the reality of that redemption in his own person in the concluding verse of the Galatian writing: "From henceforth let no man trouble me, for I bear in my body the marks of the LORD Jesus", literally meaning the brand marks as slaves were branded (Gal.6:17). They answered to the tenterhooks on which Christ the Son of God and redeemer of men, was hanged. Christ's marks were the marks of a secured redemption for all in bondage to sin: Paul's marks were the marks of a procured redemption through faith in Christ's blood.

Secondly, Paul had been born as well as bought into the household of God (Ephes.2:19) as surely as the 318 trained servants of Abraham had been born in his own house (Gen.14:14). Of himself he recalled, "But when it pleased God, who separated me from my mother's womb, and called me by His grace, to reveal His Son in me, that I might preach Him among the heathen" (Gal.1:15–16). Both the ideas of 'bought' and 'born' are aired in the colloquy between Paul and a surprised Claudius Lysias the Roman Tribune upon Paul speaking to him in the universal language of Greek. Claudias strongly queried Paul's claim to Roman citizenship, and expressed his strong doubts inferentially in his assertion, "With great sum obtained I this freedom". Paul's reply must have astounded him: "But I was freeborn". Both sides of the coin of redemption are set forth in these two statements, and are connoted in the redemption of sinners. "A truly redeemed person is bought and born", as Dr Martyn Lloyd-Jones admirably said.

Paul's calibre of service was A1, and he asserted that he was neither a hireling nor a menial who served for hire or wage, but that he served God with his spirit in the Gospel of His Son (Romans 1:9). Many there are who serve with their bodies but their hearts are not in the work, not unlike the schoolboy who drags himself to school with leaden feet, but as soon as the dismission bell rings he dashes home as with winged feet. Job likened the vanity and want of purpose of his afflictions to the servant and hireling whose labours are irksome, saying, "As a servant earnestly desireth the shadow, and as a hireling looketh for the reward of his work: So am I made to possess months of vanity" (Job 7:2–3). Their derisory name is 'clock watchers'.

In Proverbs it says that there are certain things that are never satisfied and Wesley said: "The fire that burned in Paul also never said 'It is enough'" (Prov.30:15–16). His labours extended from Jerusalem to Illyricum and round about, and far from calling it a day he proposed to enlarge his parish, first to Rome and from thence to Spain, saying, "Whensoever I take my journey into Spain I will come to you" (Rom.15:19,24). Whatever Paul put his hand to he put his heart into like the stonemason of whom it was said, "He put his conscience into every stone he laid", or better still, like the Hebrew slave who refused his freedom granted by the ceremonial law in Israel and publicly confessed, "I love my master; I will not go out free". Consequently, his ear was bored to the post of the door with a bradawl, signifying his willing and perpetual bond service to the master of that house. Paul's ear, speaking metaphorically, was as an obedient ear bored to the post of the cross of Christ, which is the door into the house or kingdom of God. Henceforth he wrote, "Let no man trouble me for I bear in my body the brands of the LORD Jesus" (Gal.6:17) – a hole in the ear denoting his willing obedience that responded to the demands of his crucified Saviour and LORD.

* *

SERMON 12

FAITH VERSUS UNBELIEF

Acts 27:25: *Wherefore, sirs, be of good cheer: for I believe God, that it shall be even as it was told me.*

The traumatic episode of the storm-tossed vessel was the direct result of the unbelief of almost everyone on board. Paul had given warning of a severe gale, with the serious loss of the ship and its cargo, as well as of their lives. Of this gale warning the master of the ship was sceptical, and was confident they could reach the port of Phenice, about twenty-five miles further along the coast of Crete. Unbelief got the vote, with fatal results.

Here is an expression of the paucity of faith, in that, apart from Luke and Aristarchus, Paul had few supporters to his counsel that they should stay and winter in the Fair Havens. All were for pressing on. So demanding is the cause of Christ, that His disciples asked the LORD, "Are there few that be saved?" He answered their question by propounding the lesson of the broad and narrow ways. One was the broad and popular way ending in destruction; the other the narrow way frequented by the minority but leading to life, of which Christ remarked, "And few there be that find it" (Matt.7:14). Only eight people, including himself, believed Noah the preacher of righteousness so that the day he and his family entered the ark "the flood came and destroyed them all" (Luke 17:27, Gen.7:11,13). Of the population of Sodom only three survived the fire and brimstone that rained from heaven. Lot was actually mocked by his own family such as his sons-in-law, who disdained his personal warning, if not entreaty.

Here we can see an expression of the paucity of faith as Paul had few supporters, other than Luke and Aristarchus, to his counsel to stay put and winter in the Fair Havens. "When the Son of Man cometh will He find faith on the earth?" (Luke 18:8), and not merely in quantity but in quality, which is elsewhere defined as "The faith which works by love" (Gal.5:6). A further answer to the question is latent in Christ's letter to the Laodicean church: "Thou thinkest that thou art rich, and increased with goods, and have need of nothing; and knowest not that thou art wretched, and miserable, and poor, and blind, and naked: I counsel thee to buy of Me gold tried in the fire, that thou mayest be rich" (Rev.3:17–18). True and tried faith called gold, purified in the fire, was at a premium in the Laodicean church. Their deceptive gold was fool's gold or feigned faith, and well illustrated by the brazen shields with which King Rehoboam replaced the golden shields of Solomon, which Shishak king of Egypt removed after his conquest of Israel (1 Kings 14:25–8). Brass, of course, strongly resembles gold in weight and appearance.

Faith's advocates are bold to confess it. Paul made his confession of his confidence in God's promise standing in the centre of the subdued ship's company. David's convictions were of like calibre and he wrote, "I believe, therefore have I spoken", with whom Paul identified and wrote, "We also believe and therefore speak" (2 Cor.4:15). Above the howling of the wind through the rigging of the ship and the raging of the waves, Paul loudly gave vent to his convictions, which have become a confession of faith. "Wherefore, sirs, I believe God, that it shall be even as it was told me". Not a word or letter of God shall be falsified. His mode of address, "sirs", was first pointedly aimed at the guilty parties who had confuted the apostle's earlier warning. Nothing, however, seemed less likely of fulfilment. There was no let-up of the storm. When Peter asked to join his Master, who was walking on the waves of an angry sea with the ease of one who had a solid causeway beneath his feet, he was invited to come to Him, and confidently responded by walking towards Him. All went well until he was distracted by the boisterous wind and began to sink. His involuntary cry was "LORD save me", and Christ's immediate response saved the apostle, but earned the rebuke, "O thou of little faith, wherefore didst thou doubt?" (Matt.14:28– 31). Conditions in the stormy Mediterranean were much more hostile than those on the Sea of Galilee, but Paul was as calm as Peter was alarmed. Peter cried, "LORD save me"; Paul loudly called, "The LORD will save you all. Cheer up, for I believe God".

Of the 276 men on board, Paul's faith was singular. He was the only one who believed God and said so. All on board were convinced that they, with the ship, were going down to the bottom, as may be deduced from Luke's unqualified statement: "All hope that we should be saved was then taken away". Here is a classic example of one man's faith bringing deliverance to many, or for the sake of a good man of God being merciful to a company of wicked men.

Zoar was one of the five cities of the plain of the Dead Sea scheduled for destruction by fire and brimstone. Lot's prayerful appeal to God to spare it from the general holocaust planned for all the cities led to its reprieve, with the LORD's assurance, "I will not destroy the city for which thou hast spoken" (Gen 19:21–3). Only the briefest of stays in Zoar revealed to Lot that although its small-ness argued for an extension of mercy, yet it exceeded the more extensive Sodom in wickedness. It is true that he vexed his right-eous soul from day to day during his residence in Sodom. He was reluctant to leave it. Although given the strongest of warnings by the angels on a judicial errand, and urged to hasten their departure, he still lingered. And one wonders whether they would have left if the angels had not grasped all four by their hands, and virtually drawn them out. The magnitude of Zoar's wickedness can only be gauged when rather than remain, he hastened to the mountains, which he before feared, and took up his living quarters in a cave (Gen.19:30). Sometimes the vice that is packaged in wrappings of virtue is far more dangerous than the palpably threatening.

From the nature of the angel's answer to Paul, assuring the apostle that his fervent appeal had been heard, it may easily be deducted that his prayer had been all-embracing: "Lo God hath given thee all them that sail with thee". Paul had specifically asked for their salvation. Ever uppermost in Paul's mind was the eternal salvation of all. He wrote to Timothy to exhort him to "pray for all men ... this is good and acceptable in the sight of God our Saviour, who will have all men to be saved, and to come unto the knowledge of the truth" (1 Tim.2:1–4). Paul so hungered and thirsted for the souls of all who made up the ship's full complement that he willingly abstained from eating and gave himself unreservedly to praying to that end. Nothing less than their salvation of spirit, soul and body as worded in the letter to the Thessalonians could satisfy him: "I pray God your whole spirit and soul and body be preserved blameless unto the coming of our LORD Jesus Christ" (1 Thess.5:23). A godly pastor who held a high position of trust in the office block of an insurance company in a large town petitioned the LORD for all the souls of those working in that block, of which he was the head. Every person employed in that block was converted before he retired from that company. God, as it were, "had given him all those that sailed with him". In the Voyage of Life there are those who sail with us: families of which everyone is a member; the office with fellow employees; the residential block where one is domiciled; or even the college campus. So persistent and prolonged was the persecution of Charles Simeon at Cambridge that his mental stability was threatened. One day as he walked in the quadrangle, in great distress because of the calumnies of members of the faculty and graduates, he sank down under his mental burden, and cried to the LORD to speak to him. Meanwhile he pulled out his Greek Testament, which he habitually carried on his person, and was greatly struck by what he read: "And they compelled one Simeon to bear His cross". He arose an inspired man, and eventually became the minister of the Parish Church of Cambridge. His preaching brought hundreds to Christ, some of whom became ministers and missionaries, one of whom was the celebrated Henry Martin, missionary to the Indies. Simeon's funeral was attended by a thousand gownsmen. God had in effect given him "all them that sailed with him": his fellow voyagers in the storm that had threatened to drown him.

A God-fearing lady complained to her husband that she felt completely inadequate, and ill-equipped to achieve anything for God. She had a strong desire to win souls for Christ in the block of flats where she lived in Edinburgh. "My dear!" her husband said, "Tha can make good gruel" which launched her out on a mission to save her neighbours. When anyone was sick or in need of sustenance, she would take them basins of gruel, and by so doing, in her simplicity she won many of them for Christ. Her concern went much further than sentiment: her desire was to save those who sailed with her.

Although all on board were far from desirable company there were no reservations in Paul's all-inclusive prayer, which company comprised his military escort, who were coarse, if not brutal Roman soldiers. John the Baptist's counsel to the soldiers who came to his baptism was sharp and to the point: "Do violence to no man". Here we have the selfish shipmen, Paul's fellow prisoners, his friends Luke and Aristarchus and the centurion. Then there was the master and owner of the ship who was the real culprit and the cause of their present troubles. He acted as a typical worldling and know-all. He had arrogantly flouted Paul's divinely given warning. This warning was indicative of Paul's intimacy with God as God's secrets are with those that fear Him. Not only had the ship's owner belittled Paul, but much more so Paul's God, whom Paul owned and was owned by, saying, "Whose I am".

Paul's heart had a penchant for his enemies, for whom he prayed as fervently as for his friends and was in line with the sentiment expressed by the LORD on the mountainside in Galilee: "Pray for those who persecute you and despitefully use you" (Matt.5:44). Job prayed so fervently for his fair-weather friends that He answered out of the whirlwind and of the storm. After being rejected by the people who had agitated for a king and replaced him as their head, Samuel said, "God forbid that I should sin against God, in ceasing to pray for you" (1 Sam.12:23).

Real faith is contagious, and Paul's faith impinged upon the Roman centurion, who initially had been indoctrinated by the master and owner of the ship, and so prejudiced as to make light of Paul's prediction of a colossal disaster unless they laid up in port. Now the centurion's predictions performed a dramatic U turn. So convinced had he become of the apostle's inside information, received privately from his personal and all-wise God, that he gave Paul virtually the command of the ship. His respect for Paul, which he entertained from his first seeing and hearing him, had been stepped up to admiration and deference. His courtesy had taken a leap to that of co-operation with his directives, as it were, overnight. Paul the prisoner had grown to master mariner, without any qualifying ship's master's papers. Faith covers a field of knowledge far beyond the human ken.

No greater tribute could be given to the ubiquitous nature of the Word of God than that of the author of Psalm 119 who in the dissertation, whose tenor from start to finish is of many-faceted truth, declared, "Thou hast made me wiser than mine enemies: for they are ever with me. I have more understanding than all my teachers: for Thy testimonies are my meditation. I understand more than the ancients, because I keep Thy precepts" (Psalm 119:98–100).

No one could have heard greater or better news than Mary of Nazareth, who was one day confronted by Gabriel, God's ambassador, and told that she was highly favoured in that she had found favour with God. And when he further enlarged on the news, that "she would conceive in her womb and bring forth a Son, who would be called 'The Son of the Highest' and reign on the throne of His father David, that of His kingdom there should be no end" (Luke 1:26–33) she asked, "How shall this be, seeing I know not a man?"

When told that "the power of the Highest should overshadow her, and that the holy thing which shall be born of thee shall be called 'The Son of God'" her reaction was a revelation of her faith: "Be it unto me according to thy word: behold the handmaid of the LORD" (Luke 1:34, 38). Faith has otherwise been defined as "the receipt of perceived truth" (Charles Finney). Mary readily received the truth which the angel had enabled her to perceive and for this reason Elizabeth's ecstatic outburst was punctuated with three beatitudes: "Blessed art thou among women; and blessed is the fruit of thy womb; and blessed is she that believed; for there shall be a performance of those things told her by the LORD" (Luke 1:42–5). Number three beatitude was subjoined because of her own husband's unbelief when told by the same angel Gabriel that "his prayer of long standing, after many years was heard, and that he should have a son, whose name would be called John, and many of the Children of Israel would he turn to the LORD, and he would go before the LORD in the spirit and power of Elijah". To this Zacharias objected, saying he was an old man and his wife was well stricken in years (Luke 1:13–18). Gabriel replied, "I stand in the presence of God, who am sent to speak unto thee, and shew thee these glad tidings, but because thou believest not my words, which shall be fulfilled in their season, thou shalt be dumb" (Luke 1:19–20).

Mary believed the far greater thing: that of a child, the God man, without the connivance of a man: which had never happened before. Zacharias baulked at the birth of a child who would be the greatest man of his day, and made possible by a reanimating of his and his wife's reproductive organs, but he believed not, though God had caused the same thing to happen before, with Abraham and Sarah, who were of far greater age than either he, Zacharias; or Elizabeth, his wife.

Mary's faith triumphed where Zacharias' faith foundered. Paul's faith triumphed where the captain and shipowner's unbelief was confounded. Paul believed, to the dotting of the 'i's' and to the crossing of the 't's', that all God had promised would be fulfilled, like Joshua, whose faith is inferred in the catalogue of worthies (Heb.11:30–1). When he summed up the campaign that involved the conquest of Canaan he stressed that "the LORD gave unto Israel all the land which He sware to give unto their fathers; and they possessed it and dwelt therein, and the LORD gave them rest round about, according to all that He sware unto their fathers: and there stood not a man of all their enemies before them; the LORD delivered all their enemies into their hand. There failed not ought of any good thing which the LORD had spoken unto the House of Israel: all came to pass" (Joshua 21:43–5). Upon their return from their Christ-assigned itineraries the disciples handed in their glowing reports, which, when completed, elicited from the LORD a searching question: "Lacked ye anything?" and their answer, without a dissonant note, was, "Nothing, LORD".

* * * * * * * * * * * * * * * * * * * *

SERMON 13

THE ISLAND OF SALVATION

Acts 27:26: *Howbeit we must be cast upon a certain Island.*

In order for the travellers to attain their salvation from their perilous surroundings, an island in that expanse of sea had to be gained. It was imperative, and in Biblical metaphor it is a figure of the salvation that is found only in Christ. In another place in the Bible Paul likens Christ to a rock, saying, "and they drank of that spiritual rock that followed them; and that Rock was Christ" (1 Cor.10:4).

A little thought soon explains the appropriateness of the figure of speech. An island is a piece of land surrounded by water, and is therefore distinct from it. Christ's singularity distinguished Him from the rest of the world as one who is not to be compared with anyone else who ever lived or lives. Of all saints He is the holiest; of angels there is none higher. Implicit in the word 'holiness' is the idea of separation, or insularity. In contrast to the High Priest of Aaron, the Hebrew writer makes much of the matter that Christ was a High Priest of a nobler order of the King Priest Melchisedec, and was "holy, harmless, undefiled, separate from sinners, and made higher than the heavens" (Heb.7:26). Further attention is drawn to Christ's uniqueness in the Colossian epistle, where it affirms that He has the pre-eminence in all things, towering like an Everest, above all other peaks in the Himalaya range of mountains, in which He is designated "The firstborn of all creation", jointly with His being "the firstborn from the dead" (Col.1:15–18).

Compared with the great land masses called continents, islands are small and inconsiderable. So men compare Christ with the towering figures of human story – the great, like Alexander, the wise like Aristotle, the mighty like the legendary Hercules, the men of art like Michael Angelo, and the wealthy like Croesus. Christ is passed over and has no stand in this hall of fame. For thirty-three years He lived in this world, "which was made by Him, and the world knew Him not. He came unto His own, and His own received Him not" (John 1:10–11). As opposed to career hunters and reputation mongers, "He made Himself of no reputation, being made in fashion as a man, and took upon Himself the form of a servant, and became obedient unto death, even the death of the cross" (Phil.2:7–8).

His apparent inferiority, however, could not detract from His singularity, and inner strength. Millions of every generation of the last 2000 years have felt the impact of His death and resurrection, and will own their place among the millions in heaven called "an innumerable company, of all nations, and kindreds and peoples and tongues" (Rev.7:9). The common cry of that cosmopolitan company ascribes their eternal salvation to the God who sits upon the throne (Rev.7:9–10).

An island is an object of stability encircled by an immense expanse of water and instability. Because the sea is given to inconstancy and change, it is an emblem of fickleness. Its waters are restless waters to the extent that the prophet Isaiah likened the wicked to its restlessness, and observed that "the wicked are like the troubled sea which cannot rest, whose waters cast up mire and dirt" (Isaiah 57:20). Jesus Christ and His Gospel is "the same, yesterday, and today and forever" (Heb.13:8), commenting on which John Wesley opined, "He changeth not from everlasting to everlasting" which, spelled out in the Christian experience, means He is trustworthy: "Only when God's covenant with day and night breaks will His promise fail" (Jer.33:20). Mary the mother of Jesus said to the perplexed servants of the marriage feast in Cana who reported the wine failure, "Whatsoever He – that is Christ – saith unto you, do it". After living with Him for thirty years, she could not be less confident that He would disappoint neither them nor the guests (John 2:5), and her confidence was justified by the sequel of a more than adequate supply of good wine.

Paul's language was specific: "Thou must be cast upon a certain island". Of the several islands in the Mediterranean God had expressed but one only that would guarantee their salvation. The proverb: "Any port in a storm" was not admissible, and could well turn out to be more dangerous than the storm. Such was the case elucidated by the prophet Amos: "As if a man did flee from a lion and a bear met him; or he went into the house (his own house) and leaned his hand upon the wall and a serpent bit him" (Amos 5:19). Any saviour will not do it; it must be Christ, the only Saviour. Paul's fear was that the Corinthians would be drawn away from "the simplicity in Christ", that looks not away to Christ alone (2 Cor.11:3). Peter's unequivocal answer to the High Priest and members of the council who claimed that there was salvation in the Law of Moses and its observance was, "Neither is there salvation in any other whereby we must be saved", except the name of Jesus, which means Saviour (Acts 4:12).

In using the word 'must', the apostle emphasised its imperative nature, which is in the tenor of a command, and the matter becomes obligatory. 'Must' is a word which is not uncommon when speaking of salvation. Peter said, "Ye *must* be saved." Paul pressed home the truth to the young churches of Lystra, Iconium and Antioch by saying, "We *must* through much tribulation enter into the Kingdom of God" Acts (14:21–2). Another example is the gaoler of Philippi's oft-quoted cry, "Sirs, what must I do to be saved?" (Acts 16:30). Christ's famous statement addressed to Nicodemus was, "Marvel not that I said unto thee 'ye *must* be born again'" (John 3:7).

One thought only was uppermost in the minds of all on board, and that was the thought of salvation, and while the possibility of being saved was removed by the complete absence of any heavenly body for many days, yet a worldly aphorism truly says that "hope beats eternal in the human breast". What music therefore was in Paul's words which intoned there would be no loss of any man's life among them. In other words their salvation was assured and would be via a certain island which ruled out any other alternative – the island was a must!

God who planned their deliverance and the place where they would escape the fury of the storm and experience the satisfaction of grounding their sea legs on terra firma, was guarantee enough that it would be a safe haven. When God underscores the promise of deliverance He leaves nothing more to be desired. No further storm would overwhelm them in their secure refuge. They would indeed be "in the cleft of the rock, and hidden in the secret places of the stairs" (Song of Sol.2:14).

Satan's expulsion from heaven to earth was the signal to concentrate his spleen against the woman, meaning the Church, who had brought forth the man child, meaning overcomers (Rev.12–13). God's answer was to provide her with the two wings of a great eagle to assist her in her flight into the wilderness, into her place, which was a safe haven "where she is nourished for a time, times, and half a time, from the face of the dragon or serpent" (Rev.12:14).

Not to be flouted, the serpent casts out of his mouth water as a flood after the woman, and is a possible reference to a great army, bent on pursuing the woman as Pharaoh pursued Israel after their departure from Egypt. On that occasion the sea opened her mouth to swallow up Pharaoh and his crack army, of whom it was written, "and they sank like lead in the mighty waters" (Exodus 15:10), which prompted the comment, "and they saw the Egyptians no more" – except as corpses on the seashore. Help came to the woman from an unexpected quarter – which is almost the rule with God and reads, "And the earth helped the woman and opened her mouth, and swallowed up the flood, which the dragon cast out of his mouth" (Rev.12:16). A possible reference could well be to an earthquake which engulfed the huge army bent on annihilating the woman.

All those in Christ are as safe as if they were in heaven, unlike the Indian tribe which fled from a prairie fire and made for the Ohio River, which marked the boundary between their own territory and the state of Alabama. Once across the river they thought they were safe, being beyond the reach of the flames. It is reported that when they had safely crossed the river they spreadeagled themselves on the ground and clutched the grass, crying "Alabama! Alamaba!", meaning, "Here is rest! Here is rest!" Tragically, they were set upon by the warlike inhabitants that populated that section of the prairies, and were brutally massacred. Their optimism was not grounded on a sure hope, and they perished. In Christ alone is there satisfactory rest, whose invitation to come to Him is proffered to all, and warmly calls, "Come unto Me and learn of Me, for I am meek and lowly in heart, and I will give you rest. Take My yoke upon you, and ye shall find rest for your souls, for My yoke *is* easy, and My burden is light" (Matt.11:28–30).

Paul said, "We must be cast upon a certain island", as it were; they were to throw themselves upon it. In the gospels we see the multitudes following Christ from "the borders of Tyre and Sidon bringing their sick and infirm as casting them down at Christ's feet". This seemed to imply that they did not intend to be burdened with them any longer. David in the Psalms invited the righteous to cast their burdens upon the LORD and He would sustain them.

Castaways have good reason to be apprehensive when cast upon an alien shore, having no knowledge of the island upon which they have been thrown by the tide, or of the goodwill or enmity of the country. In Christ there are no such fears; His character is the acme of goodwill. Of such the inhabitants shall not say, "I am sick" (Isaiah 33:24).

A popular international preacher told the remarkable story in which an American air crew had been involved, and was the outcome of their having crashed in their plane in the eastern

Pacific. Without any real ground they imagined they had landed amongst hostile natives in whose country they had been cast. For some days they kept to the forest, but hunger eventually drove them out of hiding to make their presence known to the aboriginal natives. To their amazement, instead of finding naked savages they found a gracious and civilized community, whose standard of behaviour was far superior to the norm of theirs in sophisticated and cultured America. There was no crime, no police force, no immorality, no poverty and no hospitals. And the explanation given, when asked by the castaways, was that a missionary had come amongst them years before and left them a Bible after instructing them, which resulted in the entire community receiving Christ and His salvation with His teaching, and they said, "We have taken Christ seriously". In order to have salvation you must be cast upon a certain island "where they have taken Christ seriously".

Later it would be experienced that the certain island and its native population would receive the travellers courteously and would show them great kindness. A major criticism levelled against the LORD was that "this man receiveth sinners" (Luke 15:2), and he was thus castigated when all the publicans and sinners came to hear Him. Neither were they drawn to Him because they discerned a kindred spirit, but rather the reverse; they detected a kingly and gracious one. Although they were social outcasts, Christ with an open heart called to them with an open invitation: "He who comes to Me, I will in no wise cast out". Cast-outs, castaways and cast-offs are sure of the highest entertainment (John 6:37). George Whitfield once horrified some of his genteel hearers belonging to the Countess of Huntingdon's connection. He insisted that Christ even receives the devil's cast-offs. How true it is that Christ's heart is as open to the decadent and spiritual 'down and outs' as it is to the proud and affluent 'up and outs'. Rebekah's encounter with the steward of Abraham's household, who were the nearest relatives of the patriarch, sent her dashing home, unmindful of her water pot, like another Samaritan 1900 years later, and caused great excitement in telling of the arrival of the steward and his convoy of camels. Her brother ran to the well and extended the warmest possible welcome while promising him lavish entertainment. Laban's invitation could not have been more cordial, saying, "Come in thou blessed of the LORD, wherefore standest thou without? For I have prepared the house and room for the camels" (Gen.24:24–31). Behind the eagerness to entertain the servant and his entourage from Beer-Lahai-roi, were the costly golden earring and golden bracelets on his sister's hand. Nor could he fail to be impressed by the ten camels and their trappings, which were the equipage of a very wealthy person. Mark the contrasting receptions. Christ treated the affluent with no greater respect than He did the poor and the indigent. By and large the ship's crew and company, not excepting the soldiers, were men of coarse characters, but all were treated with equal favour.

God had planned that they would be cast upon a certain island, notwithstanding their passage would be made possible by the weather agents of wind and water, apart from which they would have soon perished by the relentless buffeting of the waves. Christ's counsel to the enquiring Nicodemus, greatly puzzled by the LORD's insistence that a person to qualify for the kingdom of heaven "must be born again", was enlarged upon with a double affirmation, "Truly, truly, I say unto thee, Except a man be born of water and of the Spirit, he cannot enter into the kingdom of God" (John 3:5). They are the two effectual agents in the generating of the new Christ-like nature. By the water Christ meant the Word of God, and it is actually stated thus by Peter, who wrote, "Being born again not of corruptible seed but of incorruptible, by the Word of God which liveth and abideth for ever" (1 Pet.1:23). Christ then explained the role taken by the Spirit, that "the wind bloweth where it listeth … so is everyone who is born by the Spirit" (John 3:8).

Christ's character-changing power through the Word of God, when applied by the Spirit of God, has been long established. None more so than that illustrated in the historical Mutiny of *The Bounty*, skippered by the notorious Captain Bligh. Fletcher Christian, the first mate, with the majority of the ship's crew, mutinied on the high seas, and consigned the captain and the remainder of the ship's company to the longboat. After taking possession of the ship the mutineers sailed to the Pitcairn Islands, off the tip of South America, knowing full well that to be caught would spell their being hanged. Their days were spent in carousing and drinking of the generous supply of liquor stored in the ship. After a while, however, they grew bored for the want of diversion. One of the crew had a Bible in the bottom of his tin trunk, and having no other form of diversion he was asked to read it to the others. Within days it was noticed that their drinking and swearing became less and less, until they ceased altogether. Soon the Holy Ghost began to convince them of their sins until every man, from Fletcher Christian down, became converted and the Pitcairn Island community became fully Christian. All this was brought about by the powerful agents of the Word and Spirit of God. Even to this day the Island's postage stamps have for their motif the picture of the Bible. Coincidently the name of the ship which bore them to the Pitcairn Islands was *The Bounty*, and was a happy reminder of God's overflowing grace, and summed up in the most famous of all Bible verses, "For God so loved the world, that He gave His only-begotten Son, that whosoever believeth in Him should not perish, but have everlasting life" (John 3:16).

* * * * * * * * * * * * * * * * * * * *

SERMON 14

THE CRUCIAL HOUR

Acts 27:27: *But when the fourteenth night was come, as we were driven up and down in Adria, about midnight the shipmen deemed that they drew near to some country.*

The travellers had endured the frightening sensation of being borne by the whimsical wind and the ship being out of control. There are few more alarming experiences than being part of a set-up that has run amok. John Wesley related such an incident in his journal. He was driving a horsedrawn carriage with a lady and two young daughters as passengers, when suddenly, for no apparent reason the horse bolted and, with the bit between its teeth, ran amok. On coming to a farm it burst through the farm gates, with barely inches between the narrow gateposts and the wheels. Dashing through the farm, it emerged through another gateway. Meanwhile the lady and her two daughters clung terrified to the sides of the carriage, crying with fear. The little girls looked helplessly to Mr Wesley, who called out to them reassuringly not to fear. On the other side of the farm buildings the road sloped down towards a cliff. Anticipating the route the horse would take, a friend ran to the exit route and began waving his arms in the middle of the road at the carriage's appearance; but there was no stopping the colt. Within yards of the sheer drop the horse stopped dead, inexplicably, certainly not due to Wesley's skill, and became calm as if nothing had happened. There can be little doubt, however, that the creature had been stirred up by the prince of the power of the air, with but one object, and that to destroy Wesley, the man he most feared throughout the whole of the kingdom. During the entire incident, Wesley wrote in his journal that he had no sensation of fear, but felt as calm as if he had been in his own study (*Wesley's Journals*).

The fourteenth night found them driven up and down in Adria, with a dramatic turn of events. One moment they were the plaything of the elements being driven back and forth like a shuttlecock. This can symbolise the alternations between hope and despair and such vagaries are not unusual before a final deliverance or the fulfilment of God's promise. Sometimes, He keeps one on one's toes to the last gasp. When Pharaoh's chief butler and baker were sequestered in the king's prison with Joseph, then a prisoner of a spate of years, Joseph must have entertained the hope that God was bringing the question of his release to a head. The discharge of the butler and baker, however, brought no relief for him, but the sour grapes of disappointed hope, always the sequel of presumptuous thinking.

Joshua's conflict with Amalek well illustrated the ding-dong nature of their destabilising lot. Amalek stung Moses and Aaron into action by their unprovoked attack upon Israel. For a time they were in the ascendant, but it was not long before Amalek fought back and reversed the trend, only to be, again, rebutted by Joshua's forces. Backward and forward the struggle continued like a see-saw until sunset, when Moses' intercession, with uplifted hands, supported by Aaron and Hur, gave the victory to Joshua and his forces. Paul the apostle enunciated the principle of successful praying upon the episode, admonishing Timothy and all addressed in the first letter bearing his title: "I will therefore that men pray everywhere, lifting up holy hands without wrath and doubting" (1 Tim.2:8).

At that juncture the shipmen came into their own: they deemed that they drew near to some country. God's spokesmen are quickly vindicated by Him. Only a verse before, Paul had with confidence spoken of an island that they would be cast upon; which island would be the means of their salvation. Paul's confident assertion would have been received with scepticism by many on board, including the majority, if not all, of the shipmen.

Their expertise and keen hearing had discerned a different sound from that of the rush of the wind through the ship's rigging and the hissing of the waves around the ship. Rather, it was the sound of waves hitting rocks and solid terrain. God was about to make good His word: deliverance was imminent and within earshot. Revival is a spiritual renewal which is usually heard before it is seen.

John the Baptist's arrival in the country around Jordan produced a predictable sensation. "The people were in expectation, and all men mused in their hearts" (Luke 3:15). His preaching had convinced them that something unusual from God was at hand which was consistent with the reflections of the apostle expressed to the Galatians: "He, therefore, that ministereth the Spirit to you and worketh miracles among you, doeth He it by the works of the Law or by the hearing of faith?" (Gal.3:5). The same principle is clearly stated in the epistle to the Romans, namely that faith comes by hearing and hearing by the Word of God (Rom.10:17). Hearing, that is, of the Gospel proclaimed, is the norm by which people receive faith, as demonstrated by the born cripple at the gate at Lystra, of whom it is written, "The same heard Paul preach who steadfastly beholding him, and perceiving he had faith to be healed, said with a loud voice, 'stand upright on thy feet', and he leaped and walked" (Acts 14:8–10). Paul perceived that he had faith to be healed, having observed that he had listened intently to the Word he was preaching and had avidly devoured it.

One of the greatest revival stories of the Old Testament is that which is framed in Elijah's documentary. A prolonged drought of three and a half years had prostrated the land to a state of famine and dearth during the reign of Ahab, who with his impious and pagan wife Jezebel had given their favours to Baal and had seduced the majority of the nation. God's response was a prolonged drought through the agency of the godly Elijah. When the assigned period of three and a half years had run its course, God commanded Elijah to present himself to King Ahab and tell him that he was about to send rain. Before doing so, however, he proposed a combat between Jehovah and Baal. Each side was to offer a sacrifice to the respective deities. And the altar whose sacrifice was owned by fire from heaven was to be accounted the one transcendent God, or as Elijah expressed it, "Let Him be God" (1 Kings 18:24). Both sides presented their burnt offerings but Jehovah demonstrated His supremacy by consuming the sacrifice of Elijah. A spontaneous and thunderous applause by the people pronounced a return of their devotion to God, and ecstatically expressed "The LORD He is the God; the LORD He is the God" (1 Kings 18:39), but God had promised to send rain, which was what the country needed, not fire. Of that they had more than they could stand, of which the parched earth and scorched trees were grim reminders. Still not a single white cloud spotted the azure blue sky.

With the death croaks of the slaughtered prophets still in his ears, Elijah turned to King Ahab – notice how those men of God gave orders to their royal peers: Paul to the centurion and Elijah to the feared Ahab. "Get thee up, eat and drink; for there is a sound of abundance of rain". No one else had heard it except Elijah (1 Kings 18:41). Nor was it a brief shower, but an abundance of rain. God was about to restore the forfeited early and the latter rain of each year to the tune of three and a half years. Three and a half years of drought demanded much more than a downpour, or, for that matter, a cloudburst. It would require solid heavy rain for several days to fill the brooks and the reservoirs and rivers. Some hours later it began, after "the heavens grew black with clouds and wind" to be followed by a great rain (1 Kings 18:44–6). Elijah had not been mistaken. Likewise Paul's confident prediction was being confirmed by the pagan crew.

It was about midnight that the shipmen were apprised of the approaching land, and it was quite remarkable that Luke was able to give the time of the crucial moment, even though from the captain down no one had a watch. Ordinarily, they would have calculated their position from the sun in the day and from the stars at night by their relative positions. Thick cloud and probably dense mist had precluded such findings, yet that the Bible should indicate the exact hour is something to ponder.

Actually this is the second incident in which an unusual event is said to have taken place at the exact hour of midnight. Both in reality and fable it represents the darkest hour, and from that hour the night gradually loses its opaqueness. The purple of midnight is the backcloth with which writers and storytellers drape the macabre scene or cloak-and-dagger episode. One of the most inspiring chapters in the Acts of the Apostles, which is not lacking in inspiration from first to last, is that of the sixteenth, which deals with the founding of the Philippian church.

After a brutal flogging by the magistrates of the city, Paul and Silas were cast without ceremony into the town prison by a meanly condescending gaoler toadying to the magistrates, who had charged him to keep them safely, which sounded like a veiled threat. He in turn appeared to derive satisfaction in carrying out the order. Without any conscience, he thrust or bundled them into a veritable black hole of the inner prison – a double precaution against their escaping – and then fastened their feet in the stocks (Acts 16:22–4). In that brutal era the stocks were adapted so as to give the maximum of discomfort. There were no considerations of mercy and many stripes or beatings and floggings were received at the hands of the magistrates.

Then, at that particular juncture, the signal of midnight was given emphasis, while the narrator disclosed that at that identical hour the apostles prayed and sang praises to God, and an invisible audience of fellow prisoners was listening with rapt wonder (Acts 16:23).

From that moment God took over the prison and convulsed it with a violent earthquake, not the expression of a natural phenomenon, but a spiritual and miraculous one: "The foundations were shaken; the doors were thrown open immediately, and everyone's bonds were loosed" (Acts 16:26). There were no casualties, not a piece of masonry fell, and no one broke gaol. God does not back criminals; nor does He encourage prison outbreaks. The same power that loosed their bonds kept them from absconding, which most probably saved the gaoler from capital punishment and thereby paying with his life for allowing the breakout. Not for nothing did "the gaoler draw his sword to take his own life" (Acts 16:27).

Even more significant than all this is the schedule of the shipmen's sensitivity to the nearness of the approaching land. Early in the story attention is drawn to another Biblical date of cardinal importance, which is the date of the Day of Atonement, when all the sins of Israel were confessed or made public, before being forgiven and put away, through the role of the scapegoat (Acts 27:9). In the story under review the fourteenth day harks back to the Day of Days in the whole range of Jewish history: in fine when the nation broke with Egypt, who for a hundred years or more had been their liege lords and they their vassals, stripped of all rights, and were everything but branded.

"At midnight the Angel of the LORD went through the land of Egypt and slew the eldest son in every home, from the king's son to that of the firstborn of the captive in prison, as well as the firstborn of cattle" (Exodus 12:29, Exodus 11:4–8).

As well as the ordinance being enacted at midnight it was carried out on the fourteenth day, and ever after became the most important of all Israel's memorial days and was to be rigidly observed in Jerusalem. Furthermore, it was spoken of as a night much to be remembered (Exodus 12:6,18). Passover night saw the nation preserved from the Angel of Death, when he visited every Egyptian home. In addition the night of the Passover saw the people being delivered from bitter bondage, and the inaugural night of their becoming a nation and no longer an heterogeneous rabble, but an homogeneous nation made up of the twelve tribes and forged together into a single entity. It was, indeed, the night of their salvation in the fullest sense, and it launched them into a new era and a new beginning, which wound up their protracted night of bondage. And to think that it began at midnight on the fourteenth night coincidental with the timing of the shipmen's discernment of the approach of land as previously predicted by the servant of God as the certain land of deliverance from the still turbulent sea.

It is hardly possible to miss the association of fourteen in other parts and events of the Bible, and the link is always with some form of deliverance, or restoration to the place and favour of God, and sometimes after clear defiance of His orders. Balak the king of Moab had set his sights on cursing Israel, and summoned Balaam from Aram to further his ill will. With an eye to the main chance and another on a lucrative reward, Balaam determined to humour his royal patron. To that end Balaam had Balak erect seven altars at three vantage points in turn and in keeping with his evil design on each of the seven altars a bullock and a ram were offered. Instead, however, of cursing, he found himself blessing Israel, to the chagrin of Balak. Notwithstanding, the devil never gives up – not until he finds himself in the Lake of Fire with his millions of duped votaries, so a similar procedure was adopted with the other pair of seven altars. Their stations only were changed. Yet no anathemas emerged from the prophet's lips. Not only was Israel greatly blessed, but each succeeding endeavour witnessed proliferating blessing in Israel's favour (Numbers 23:1–11; 14:24; 23:29–30; 24:1– 10), which makes it impossible to miss the lesson: fourteen is significant of God's goodwill and deliverance. God was greatly indignant with Eliphaz and his two friends, who had misrepresented His goodness to the patriarch, and virtually libelled the LORD. So after dealing with Job and correcting his errors of judgement, He turned to his bigoted critics and threatened them for their unkind treatment. To make amends they were commanded to take seven bullocks and seven rams and offer up the fourteen beasts for their misdemeanours and uncharitable conduct. God promised that He would hear and accept Job's intercessory prayer for them, and would pardon them, because unlike them, Job had spoken that which was right. Failure to do as He commanded them would provoke the LORD to deal with them after their folly, but the fourteen burnt offerings placated God and turned His anger from them (Job 42:7–10).

* * * * * * * * * * * * * * * * * * *

SERMON 15

TAKING SOUNDINGS: A WISE PRECAUTION

Acts 27:28: *And sounded, and found it twenty fathoms: and when they had gone a little further, they sounded again, and found it fifteen fathoms.*

An intimation of the close proximity of land coupled with complete ignorance of their bearings was sufficiently alarming to call for the use of the lead to take soundings. Within a little they would learn of their nearness to a rock-bound shore. A black night and a sky of ten-tenth cloud coverage by day would argue their using the slender means of a sounding lead.

Earlier in the tussle with the elements to help them ride out the storm or keep the vessel on an even keel, the mariners had cast away the tacklings of the ship with everything that was at that point in the voyage dispensable, but wisely held on to the casting lead. Likewise, the Christian has in the Bible or Word of God an infallible medium or guide enabling him to determine his true spiritual state at any given moment without his being under any illusions about his credit with God being any other than good. The House of the Forest of Lebanon, built by Solomon for his own state, as Hampton Court was built by Cardinal Wolsey and presented to Henry VIII as a gift, was called 'The House of the Forest of Lebanon', because the timber of which it was mainly composed – cedar and fir – was taken from Lebanon's majestic forest. Of the windows let into the walls, it is said that they were in three ranks and that light or window was over against light, which obviated any shadow (1 Kings 7:4). Thus the windows answered each other and illustrated the truth that when the heart and understanding of the believer corresponds with the LORD's, all disparity is eliminated: "That in His light we see light".

Ezekiel tested the depth of the waters flowing from under the threshold of the House of God, using his body as well as the measuring gauge as he walked the several stretches, each a thousand cubits in length. He began at ankle depth and continued to knee depth. The third thousand cubits measured up to his loins and finally the fourth stretch of a thousand cubits was too deep to be crossed. Ezekiel described them as risen waters, or otherwise defined as "waters to swim in". His feet failed to touch the bottom (Ezek.47:4–5). Correspondingly, by comparing our daily walk with the sounding lead of the Word of God, it is not a complicated matter to come to a fairly accurate conclusion of our spiritual status, in other words the depth or shallowness of our experience in our walk with God.

King Josiah was the last of a mere handful of godly kings who ruled in Judah. One of his first actions was to repair and purge the neglected and dilapidated House of God. While carrying out these renovations Hilkiah the High Priest found the Book of the Law in the House of the LORD: it had lain in the side of the Ark (Deut.34:26), neglected by a succession of kings, and surprisingly it is problematic whether even Solomon had paid much attention to it. Had he done so his reign would not have tailed off so dismally, especially after having written out a copy and placing it in the pocket or pouch in the side of the Ark. That very book commanded every king who ascended the throne to write out a copy of it, and enjoined reading it as well. It may be concluded that not even the exemplary Hezekiah carried out the divine charge (Deut.17:18–20).

The book of Deuteronomy, which is the copy of the Law referred to and was incumbent upon the kings to transcribe, expressly prohibited kings from multiplying horses, multiplying wives, or greatly multiplying silver and gold. Solomon was more culpable than any other Israelitish monarch in these areas. Either he was blatantly rebellious or was so negligent as totally to ignore the injunction "to read therein all the days of his life" (Deut.17:19).

Josiah's grief was so great that he rent his clothes and humbled himself to the lowest degree, and followed up his deep act of contrition by a thorough purgation of idols from the land, including Samaria, though long since shorn of her kings. Predictions concerning sweeping the deck clean of all idolatry, which went back to the reign of the first Jeroboam, were carried out to the letter (1 Kings 13:2). When Josiah used the sounding lead of God's Word, it was the moment of truth and clearly revealed the shallowness of the nation, Samaria included. Despite the severity of the reforms and their sweeping nature, they were too late to stave off a national disaster. One crumb of comfort, however, was, vouchsafed Josiah, that the national judgement and desolation would not be implemented during his reign (2 Kings 22:8–20).

Every Breaking of Bread service is a divinely given opportunity to take soundings, as well as a memorial service of the LORD's death. On the eve of His departure from this world in the form of a violent and horrendous death, He gave directions to commemorate it by eating symbolically broken bread and drinking wine from a common cup, and added by way of explanation, "For as often as ye eat this bread and drink this cup ye do show the LORD's death till He come". This was followed by a clear injunction that also contained a solemn warning: "Wherefore let a man examine himself, and so let him eat and so let him drink. For he that eateth and drinketh unworthily" after failing to pass the test standard required by God "eateth and drinketh damnation to his own soul" (1 Cor.11:23–31).

Much more so if there has been slackness or lethargy and carelessness in the performance of public duties. Peter's agonised outburst to the LORD: "Depart from me for I am a sinful man O LORD" must have puzzled if not disturbed the other apostles (Luke 5:8). Although a little thought soon explains Peter's outburst, his offer to let down the net out of deference to Christ smacked of hypocrisy. Ostensibly he was being obedient to Christ's command, but it was a feigned obedience. Christ had commanded to put down 'net**s**'; Peter let down only one. His undemurring unbelief reasoned that one net would be sufficient to discredit Christ's judgement, when actually they required not two nets but two boats; for they – Andrew and Peter – beckoned to their partners James and John, who were in the other ship, to help them land the catch. Christ the Living Word and spiritual sounding lead revealed the true state of a spiritually complacent Peter.

Only by monthly stocktaking of checking his wares left on the shelves after a month's trading can a vendor keep a tally of his sales, and by the regular stocktaking detect fraudulent practice and dishonesty among his staff, and only by doing this regularly and systematically would he have any notion of whether he was solvent or bordering on bankruptcy. A clear moral points itself: don't take it for granted that everything is all right: rather make it one's practice to take soundings.

Even the best of people need to observe the above rule. In Bible days it would have been difficult to have found two more responsible persons than Mary and Joseph; at least God thought so by choosing them to be the custodians of the World's Saviour in childhood. Gabriel's' communication to Mary was "Fear not Mary for thou hast found favour with God" (Luke 1:30). After the yearly Passover Feast at Jerusalem they made their way home, to make the distressing discovery that Christ was not with them, although they had supposed He was among the company of family and friends who travelled together. A whole day had elapsed before they missed Him, but when they took soundings, that is, made enquiries, they came face to face with the shuddering reality that the child Jesus had been left behind. No greater loss had ever been made by anyone in this world, which, of course, is true of anyone who loses Christ and His salvation. For three days they searched before finding Him in the Temple precincts holding intelligent conversation with "the learned doctors of the Law" (Luke 2:46).

When duty bound, if something has to be left behind let it be your wallet rather than the Word of God, of which there is no surer instrument for taking soundings. Before the duty is satisfactorily carried out, it might well spell someone's salvation, as well as one's own, even "all those that sail with you". A pastor of a thriving fellowship recently introduced me at an induction service to a young lady, who was with his wife. She had barely arrived from Swaziland, when within a few days of her arrival she saw a person carrying a bible on his way to church. That bible alerted her to a spiritual need in her life. Not only did she follow him into the church, but thereupon gave her life to Christ. She was saved by a 'depth sounder'. Perhaps the sight of the book, with which she had been once familiar, stirred the depths within her.

Paul wrote to the Corinthians, saying, "Examine yourselves, whether ye be in the faith; prove your own selves. Know ye not your own selves, how that Jesus Christ is in you, except ye be reprobates?" (2 Cor.13:5) The crucial matter with the Corinthians was whether they had the witness of Christ within them, which expressed itself by the inner awareness of the fruits of the Spirit of Christ, instinct in the nature of Christ, or as the writer cogently declares in another of his writings, "Now if any man have not the Spirit of Christ, he is none of His" (Rom.8:9), and in the same chapter, "The Spirit itself beareth witness with our spirit, that we are the children of God" (Rom.8:16). In other words, the test conspires to the certainty of "Christ in you, the hope of glory" (Col.1:27). Where such is lacking leads to exclusion, or becoming a reprobate, unable to stand the test, and inevitably becoming a castaway.

Sadly there are some who flinch from the sounding lead, and avoid certain preachers whose searching sermons make them feel uncomfortable. How much better to face the harsh truth and make the adjustments required by the Word of God. Saul of Tarsus was subject to the goad of the Word of God, piercing his conscience deeply, in his endeavours to resist the truth of Christ and salvation through a cursed cross, wisely submitted in words that conceded complete surrender: "LORD what wilt Thou have me to do?" (Acts 9:6). How different the adverse reaction of Felix, who could not conceal his perturbation or his physical agitation, when Paul applied the sounding lead to his life and conscience in his impromptu diatribe and "reasoned of righteousness, temperance and judgement to come" (Acts 24:25). He had heard more than he had bargained for, and could stand no more, and abruptly dismissed him. How much wiser it is to bear present discomfort and to be spared eternal shipwreck, which will be the lot of a reprobate.

A lovely story told of Mary Slessor, called 'The White Queen of Calabar', who served God with distinction in that part of Africa, well illustrates the moral courage of steadfastness under pressure, sometimes called grit. A gang of louts surrounded her as she came out of a church in her native Scotland. One of them was whirling a piece of metal on a cord around his head in ever-widening circles, and inching closer and closer to her face, but she neither moved nor flinched and thereby won their admiration. She had passed their nerve-racking test. Their lead sounded her and she came through the ordeal to – I understand – win them for the LORD and many more in Calabar.

Every beekeeper examines his brood chambers to determine that a newly formed queen bee isn't about to swarm with a swarm comprising thousands of bees. Such would be a disaster.

The travellers safety depended upon the depth of water beneath the keel. More vessels are sunk in shallow water than in the ocean depths. Sir Francis Drake, after going around the world involving four years at sea, ran into a storm in the Thames estuary and was within a very little of being wrecked, and expressed his feelings by succinctly crying out, "Have I been round the world safely, come home to be drowned in a ditch?"

They threw the lead over the gunwale and registered twenty

fathoms, at which depth there was no danger, which has its own lesson. Twenty in Bible numerology equates to confirmed holiness. Two is the number of confirmation. Twenty equals ten times two – or God's Law confirmed. His Law or Ten Commandments bespeaks His standard of holiness. Zechariah among his several visions saw a flying roll measuring twenty times ten cubits, and it represented the curse of God going forth over all the earth (Zech.5:1–3). In so doing, it is said, to cut off on one side the thief and on the other side those who swear falsely. The one sins against his neighbour and the other, the false swearer, sins against God. It was destined to enter and remain in the house of the thief and on the other side to remain in the house of the one who commits perjury against God, who swears falsely in His name. In each such house the scroll would remain until it consumed the house with the timber and stones.

Holiness is demanded by God; it is the reflex of His character and of His glory, which is defined as the out-shining of God's character, who declares that "without which no man shall see the LORD" (Heb.12:14). God's universal censure is that, "all have sinned and fall short of the glory of God" (Rom.3:23). In spite of God's charge and incumbent upon all: "Be ye holy for I am holy", and again "Be ye holy as I am holy" (1 Pet.1:15–16), the self-evident fact is that all have missed the mark and fallen short of the image of God. Notwithstanding, God has provided the answer in Christ, "Being justified freely by His grace through the redemption that is in Christ Jesus" (Rom.3:23 –25).

When a second sounding was taken it was revealed there was a discrepancy of five cubits from that of the first and revealed a current depth of fifteen cubits, which was a clear indication that the seabed was rapidly shelving, and warned of imminent peril.

Fifteen is the number of the grace of God. Five is the recognised number of grace. We see this at the pool of Bethesda where the 'House of Mercy' was made up of five porches. Fifteen represents three-fold grace as in the grace of the 'Three-in-One

God'. God's grace, as generally understood, is the expression of His undeserved or unmerited love. At the heart of the Gospel is the satisfaction that "where sin abounds grace doth much more abound" (Rom.5:20).

In the story of Noah's Ark it is contended that the Ark was borne up by the waters of judgement fifteen cubits above the highest mountain. Those mountains can only but represent the mountains of sin of the world, but topped by the waters of grace which carry the family of Noah fifteen fathoms clear, and this is an apt demonstration that where sin abounds, grace doth much more abound. Fifteen fathoms of water, therefore, kept the Ark clear above the world. This truth was emphasised by Peter, who stated that few, that is, eight souls were saved by water, and delivered from the old world and its untoward generation (1 Pet.3:20). This peculiar virtue is stressed by repetition in the second chapter of the Ephesian epistle: "Therefore by grace are ye saved through faith … Not of works, lest any man should boast" (Ephes.2:8,9). With fifteen fathoms of water beneath the keel there is no danger. Beyond that point, however, there is certain disaster. With this in mind the Hebrew writer urged the runners in the Christian race to "lift up the hands which hang down, and strengthen the feeble knees. Follow peace with all men and holiness without which no man shall see the LORD: looking diligently lest any man fail of the grace of God" (Heb.12:13– 15). A clear unequivocal directive is to "give diligence" – literally to make it one's whole concern – "lest any man fail of the grace of God" (Heb.12:15).

To fall short of the glory of God is serious, but not unredemptive: grace is readily available to make up the shortfall, "to deny ungodliness and worldly lust and to live soberly, and righteously and godly in this present world, looking for that blessed hope and the glorious appearing of the great God and our Saviour Jesus Christ, who gave Himself for us that He might redeem us from all iniquity, and purify unto himself a peculiar people, zealous of good works" (Titus 2:11–14).

In marked contrast, to fall short of the grace of God has no remedy: "He that despised Moses' law died without mercy under two or three witnesses: Of how much sorer punishment, shall he be found worthy, who hath trodden under foot the Son of God, and hath counted the blood of the Son of God, wherewith he was sanctified, an unholy thing, and hath done despite unto the Spirit of grace?" (Heb.10:28–9).

Fifteen fathoms is the limit of God's forbearance: there is not only danger but death beyond this point: it is time to put down the anchors.

* * * * * * * * * * * * * * * * * * *

SERMON 16

ROCKS AND ANCHORS

Acts 27:29: *Then fearing lest we should have fallen upon rocks, they cast four anchors out of the stern, and wished for the day.*

Life's voyage is never wanting in its alternations of danger. The travellers' first hazard was the quicksands, the notorious Sirtis off the North African coast, of which they were in trepidation of falling foul. Now, a fortnight later, they were equally as apprehensive of rocks which were uncomfortably close, although hidden from sight. Dangers can assume contrasting forms but equally forbidding: quicksands comprise millions of minute particles of sand or fragmented rock, while rocks are large and towering, yet the one hazard is no less to be feared than the other. It is true, even so, that more ships are wrecked on rocks than are grounded on shoals to be battered by waves.

On the sea of life there are rock hazards of various types. Christ is the true and only Rock of Ages. Isaiah's exhortation has its inspiration from this idea: "Trust ye in the LORD for ever, for in the LORD Jehovah is everlasting strength" – literally "a Rock of Ages" (Isaiah 26:4).

In his farewell address to Israel before climbing Mount Nebo, from which God would remove him into His presence, Moses, in a searching speech, reminded them of the many times they had been unfaithful to God and had defaulted to other gods, and in so doing had turned their back on God the Rock of their salvation, despite these nations actually conceding that such gods are lesser and inferior beings. They who were their enemies were their judges saying, "For their Rock is not as our rock" (Deut.32:3).

In His celebrated Olivet discourse, and delivered immediately to His disciples after His final leave-taking of the Jewish ordinances and Temple worship, having evoked His anathema upon them, Christ ranged at large on the monumental happenings which would be a run-up to the end of the world. Especial stress was laid upon the emergence of false Christs, followed by the appearance of spurious prophets. Towards the close of the discourse He returned to the theme and disclosed that a plurality of counterfeit Christs and pseudo prophets would present their credentials of extraordinary signs of wonders, whose motive was to deceive and destroy if possible the whole body of Christ's elect (Matt.24:5,11, 24). Literally, they would simulate Christ the eternal Rock (1 Cor.10:4), and present themselves as a phalanx of rocks to shipwreck the Faith and destroy the souls of the believers. Always it seems that the parting addresses of God's servants have been punctuated with warnings of the desperate designs of the enemies of God to scuttle those who are heavenward bound. Paul's farewell to the Ephesian elders delivered at Miletus was of a similar vein, when he sorrowfully said, "For I know that after my departing shall grievous wolves enter in among you, not sparing the flock" (Acts 20:27) and wolves at large among the flock will scatter and devour it. God's flock, as it were, marooned upon the rocks.

The appearance of Barnabas and Saul at Paphos in Cyprus involved them in a fracas with one self-styled Bar-Jesus, but surnamed Elymas, meaning 'sorcerer'. The apostles had been invited by Sergius Paulus, the deputy of the country, to expound the Word of God and while doing so Elymas withstood them. Prior to the arrival of the apostles, this sorcerer had basked in the patronage of the governor. He angrily reacted to the heavenly messenger and sought to turn away the Roman deputy from the faith, which was far more serious than refuting their message. From the favourable impression that Paul and Barnabas had made upon Sergius Paulus it was evident Elymas was in danger of losing a client. To prevent this Paul pointedly called the sycophant "a Child of the Devil" in apposition to what he called himself: "child or son of Jesus", by which he exactly answered the description of a false Christ or prophet. Paul's severe castigation anathematised Elymas as "an enemy of all righteousness whose chief object was to pervert the right ways of the LORD" (Acts 13:10). But for this timely and sweeping judicial action, the faith of the governor would have been wrecked in its early stages. Instead it received a powerful boost (Acts 13:12).

Jude admonishes "the saints to contend earnestly for the faith" in his brief but revealing writing (Jude 3). He disclosed that certain men had clandestinely joined their fellowship. Among other features he declared that "they were spots in their feasts of charity" (verse 12), literally "they were sunken rocks in their love feasts". Needless to say, sunken rocks are more to be feared, for much more dangerous – for less suspected – than "frowning beetling ones". Judas Iscariot was a sunken rock, yet probably of the twelve apostles, the least suspected of treachery.

Men's hearts are often likened to rocks in their obduracy and hardness, of which the hardening element is unbelief. God pronounced the whole body of Israelites in the desert as being rock-hardened, and held them up to reprehension to all subsequent generations of Jews, whose wickedness was to be avoided. God's blistering censure was: "Harden not your hearts as in the provocation, in the day of temptation in the wilderness" (Heb.3:8) and again, "With whom was He grieved forty years? Was it not with them that had sinned and whose carcases fell in the wilderness?" (Heb.3:17)

Without controversy the supreme example of a rock-hardened heart is that of Pharaoh, as recorded in the book of Exodus, but from whom many salutary lessons are drawn elsewhere in the Bible, particularly the New Testament. After his co-operating with God's emissaries Moses and Aaron in the releasing of Israel from decades of bondage, he became hardened yet again. Already his hardness of heart had involved the death of the firstborn son in every Egyptian family, but he seemed to have learned nothing from the relentless judicial punishment that had fallen upon his subjects.

With the cream of his army he gave hot pursuit and overtook Israel between Pi-hahiroth and Baal-zephon, the former name meaning 'the openings of liberty', which was a suitable name to explain Israel's experience as they were beginning to enjoy the fruits of liberty. Moses' uplifted rod assuaged Israel's alarm when a swathe of solid ground was opened up through the watery expanse by which the people pressed on, into which Pharaoh also was decoyed. His rage had hardened him to the wonder of the enactment, even as but forty years hence Balaam's anger against his ass would blind him to the miracle of a talking donkey. When Pharaoh's army was trapped between watery walls, and his chariots bogged down, for the second time during that epic event, Moses raised his rod and the waters returned to their normal bed, and the reading runs, "And the LORD overthrew the Egyptians in the midst of the sea" (Exodus 14:21, 26, 27). Moses and Israel made much of the Egyptians' disastrous eclipse, and used striking and appropriate imagery to the effect that "the depths have covered them: they sank into the bottom as a stone" (Exodus 15:5). Nor could the wording have been more apt. Pharaoh's heart was as adamant, which was a rock indeed, while the hearts of his cohorts had become flint-like in their opposition to God. Pharaoh's contagious hardness had petrified theirs, and they sank together as one cemented rock.

"Fearing rocks" is a timely reminder to all bound together in the voyage of life and advised so by the author of the Hebrew epistle, "Take heed brethren, lest there be in any of you an evil heart of unbelief, in departing from the Living God, but exhort one another daily, while it is called today, lest any of you be hardened through the deceitfulness of sin" (Heb.3:12–13).

The stone of a hard heart is a stone of stumbling and a rock of offence to the renewal of a dead fellowship or the revival of a dead and barren ministry. As long as the stone blocks the entrance, the dead Lazarus will remain entombed. Christ's command is decisive: "Take ye away the stone" (John 11:39). A failure to remove the hard heart keeps the glory of God in quarantine, but the very moment the stone was taken away from the place where the dead was laid, at the LORD's strident command "he that was dead came forth bound hand and foot with grave-clothes" (John 11:44). Only faith can melt the hard heart and reveal the glory of God. Christ clearly stated the terms: "Martha, said I not unto thee, that if thou wouldest believe, though shouldest see the glory of God?" (John 11:40)

With expedition they cast four anchors out of the stern and waited for the daylight to determine their next move. An anchor is a consistent emblem of hope, which is said to be an innate part of the Christian character, which is briefly but fully summed up in Paul's brilliant aphorism: "And now abideth faith, hope and charity, these three; but the greatest of these is charity" (1 Cor.13:13).

No ship would set sail without an anchor. With storms contributing to the normal pattern of seafaring, an anchor is an indispensable part of the tackling of a ship. Its one and only function is to secure the ship from drifting when in port or near shore, and prevents the disaster of being wrecked. What brakes are to a road vehicle, anchors are to seagoing craft. Julias Cæsar's invasion of Britain almost met with a premature disaster. Coming from a country and a sea coast where there is no tide, he did not bother to anchor his fleet off the coast of Britain, and before the Romans realized it, their fleet began to be carried out to sea. Life's turbulence and crises demand means which will counteract drifting and offset calamity and despair, which is the proper function of the anchor of hope, and is fully qualified to do.

Hope's province is always the future, in contrast to the chequered past, for it is always bound up with good and happiness, as distinct from sorrow and failure and despair. Moreover, it has well been observed that it influences the present because of the future.

Four anchors represent the four Gospels, or Christ who is the universal hope and salvation; four is the number of the world. In the four Gospels Christ is set forth in His four different roles or aspects of salvation, and is adverted to as our hope and in whom also is our hope. This dual aspect is presented in the Hebrew letter where the writer succinctly remarks, "That by two immutable things, in which it was impossible for God to lie, we might have a strong consolation, who have fled for refuge to lay hold upon the hope set before us: Which hope we have as an anchor of the soul, both sure and steadfast, which entereth into that within the veil; Whither the forerunner is for us entered, even Jesus, made a High Priest for ever after the order of Melchisedec" (Heb.6:18–20). "Those who have fled to Christ have strong consolation, swallowing up all doubt and fear, after being tossed by many storms to lay hold of the hope set before us, that is on Christ the object of our faith, and the glory we hope for through Him" (John Wesley).

While the hope is one entity, it is presented in Christ in a four-faceted way, hence the four Gospels, and the forte of that hope is the resurrection of Christ. Peter wrote: "Blessed be the God and Father of our LORD Jesus Christ, which according to His abundant mercy who hath begotten us again unto a lively hope by the resurrection of Jesus Christ from the dead" (1 Peter 1:3). Each of the four Gospels lays the greatest stress on Christ's resurrection, and brings the message and history of Christ's life and purpose to a band-storming and fitting climax by its narration. It is no overstatement to insist that the resurrection is the Gospel. All the threads of divine truth and doctrine come together in the resurrection of Christ. Paul frequently alluded to it and its spiritual significance. He inevitably gave it the place of pre-eminence. Typical of such is his opening salvo, in his definition of the Gospel, with its centrality of the cross and resurrection, and his subsequent list of witnesses of the historical fact, accompanied by indubitable proof.

Finally it is capped by the experimental and practical outworking of the present power of Christ's resurrection (1 Cor.1–8).

Beginning the above chapter the apostle wrote: "For I have preached unto you the Gospel ... by which also ye are saved ... For I delivered unto you first of all ... how that Christ died for our sins according to the Scriptures; And that He was buried, and that He rose again the third day according to the Scriptures" (1 Cor.15:1–4).

The prophet Jonah's epic experience of his being swallowed by a whale and of being vomited after three days' incarceration was deliberately designed by God to highlight the greatest of all Gospel signs. The religious fraternity of Christ's day constantly harped on their being given a special sign to endorse Christ's claim to the validity of His eternal Sonship, only to be told that no sign would be forthcoming except that of the prophet Jonah: "As Jonah was three days and three nights in the whale's belly, so the Son of Man would be three days and three nights in the heart of the earth".

This anchor, with its four-faceted presentation of Christ as King by Matthew, as the Faithful Servant by Mark, the representative Son of Man by Luke, and the celestial Son of God by John, is a sheet anchor indeed, and, being portrayed in this four-fold way, guarantees universal hope. In *Hebrews* it states "which hope we have as an anchor of the soul, both sure and steadfast" and has never been known to drag. With consummate ease it can offset the pull of all contrary winds and adverse tides and currents and has an untarnished reputation for being rockproof. No one who ever depended upon its stability wrecked their faith. Among the medley of epithets that establish His pre-eminence, the hope anchor is called: "a Lively Hope" (1 Pet.1:3), "a Blessed Hope" (Titus 2:13), "a Purifying Hope" (1 John 3:3), "a Glorious Hope" (Col.1:27), and "a Good Hope" (2 Thess.2:16).

What egregious folly it would have been had the sailors cast away their anchors when earlier they lightened the ship. It is not without reason that the believer is appealed to, "to cast not away his confidence which hath great recompense of reward" (Heb.10:35).

It is expressly said that "they cast four anchors out from the stern of the boat" (verse 29). Their immediate danger was from the rear. Had they cast the anchors from the prow or bow there was more than a real possibility of the stern of the boat being swept around by the waves and a side wind with the gale alternating and changing direction and landing them on the rocks.

So it is that man's greatest danger is from behind or from one's past. Paul, with great pains, pointed this out to the Ephesian believers: "Wherein, in time past ye walked according to the course of this world, according to the prince of the power of the air, the spirit that no worketh in the children of disobedience and were by nature the children of wrath, even as others" (Ephes.2:1–3). Indeed their history was bleak. Continuing in a similar drift, Paul appealed to them to turn back the calendar. "Remember ye being in times past Gentiles in the flesh, that at that time, ye were without Christ, being aliens from the commonwealth of Israel, and strangers from the covenants of promise, having no hope, and without God in the world" (Ephes.2:12). It is hardly possible to envisage a more desperate plight than being without God and without hope. No hope spells no future: no God equates to no help in the present. How unlike the writer of Psalm 46: "God is our refuge and strength; a very present help in trouble" (Psalm 46:1). Better that such people had never been born, like Absalom and Judas. Graciously the Gospel interposes a salvaging 'but': "But now in Christ Jesus, ye who were sometimes far off are made nigh by the blood of Christ" (Ephes.2:13).

First of all the Gospel has to deal effectively with our past by obliterating it, and unless it is completely erased it will ruin us, on the insistence of the Bible's indictment by an accusing past and by the logical sequel a damning one. By parity of thought the Day of Judgement has to do with a person's past, and there can be no more disquieting thought than on that day every person will be faced with their past life and will be like a reproduction of a once-popular television programme, *This Is Your Life*, with one unpleasant difference: with the television programme nothing adverse or discrediting is included – it comprises pleasant and flattering happenings. In the real run of one's life on the time screen, every detail will be brought into the script; bad, good and indifferent; the known and the unknown details; one's thought pattern, and public deportment. It would be no exaggeration to say that most people would rather confront their worst enemy than their past.

Before introducing the new heaven and the new earth "God will require that which is past" (Eccles.3:16). This consideration of man's past with its impact upon his eternal future, to boot, is dramatically presented in the predicted destiny of Dan the son of Jacob. His citation reads, "Dan shall be a serpent by the way, an adder in the path, that biteth the horse's heels so that his rider shall fall backward" (Gen.49:17). Dan means judgement which deals with the past, and aptly it is said to bite the back part of the heel, and this being his Achilles tendon is the weakest and most vulnerable part. When thus stricken the horse rears upon its haunches and throws its rider backward. At the Judgement, Dan – the heavenly judge, namely the Son of Man: "The man whom God hath ordained, and by whom He will judge the world in righteousness; and hath given assurance to all men, in that He hath raised Him from the dead" (Acts 17:31) will throw every person in the world back on his past, and thereupon "require that which is past". And no truth drug will be needed.

"...And wished for the day". To be enveloped in darkness and simultaneously to be sensible of danger in very close proximity is nothing if not nerve-racking, which could not be better illustrated than by the experience of the Christian young woman who had been beaten unconscious and thrown into a pit, which was as black as pitch. Upon regaining consciousness she was made aware of a snake coiled on her stomach, though she could not see it. Nothing more terrifying could possibly be imagined. Isaiah's words could never be more seasonable: "Who is among you that feareth the LORD, that obeyeth the voice of His servant, that walketh in darkness and hath not light? Let him trust in the name of the LORD, and stay upon his God" (Isaiah 50:10). As she obeyed the heavenly counsel, heavenly help was sent her, and an angel of light lifted her, less one snake, out of the devil's snake pit.

"Light is sown for the righteous" (Psalm 97:11), and will spring up to reassure them and quieten all their fears, even as it sprang up in the prison of Herod, where Peter was sleeping soundly between two soldiers, when the angel of the LORD came upon him, and a light shined in the prison" (Acts 12:7). "Now, indeed, we know in part, then shall we know even as we are known" (1 Cor.13:12).

Every believer could desire more than any day, the Day of the LORD, alias the Eternal Day, and "the Day when there shall be no more sea" (Rev.21:1). Incredible as it sounds, the matrix of the sea will give birth to no more cloud or storm, or trouble or tears, but "God shall be all and in all" (1 Cor.15:28). May that day break soon. "Let there be light" (Gen.1:3).

* * * * * * * * * * * * * * * * * * * *

SERMON 17

A FALSE COLOUR OF HYPOCRISY EXPOSED

Acts 27:30: *And as the shipmen were about to flee out of the ship, when they had let down the boat into the sea, under colour as though they would have cast anchors out of the foreship.*

A false colour of hypocrisy is a deliberately misleading action which ostensibly is a virtuous one, but masks an evil or vicious one, as of old, pirates or rum runners were wont to fly an honoured flag before falling upon and boarding an unsuspecting vessel carrying a rich cargo. When their rich prize was secured they would haul down the honoured flag and replace it with the skull and crossbones. In the same way guns would be camouflaged and only exposed when within firing range of their intended prize.

Ocean-going vessels trailed a longboat to ferry their crew and passengers from the ship to the shore or harbour, and this could act as a lifeboat when the mothership was in distress or in danger of sinking. Fully persuaded that the vessel would sink before reaching shore or port, they made stint to save their own skins by using the auxiliary boat to close the distance between them and the land by a speedy dash for safety. They probably reasoned that their keelless boat stood a fair chance of making the shore in a boisterous sea.

Not daring to reveal their true purpose, their pretext was of dropping additional anchors at the prow or bow of the ship to bolster the four at the stern. A law of the sea is that the crew are the last to leave a sinking ship, and even in modern times the captain is armed with a gun to prevent anyone countermanding

LESSONS FROM THE VOYAGE OF LIFE

that rule, but the Egyptian crew of this grain ship had no such scruples. Earlier on in this saga of the sea it was related how they struggled to secure the trailing boat and hoist it onto the deck; they had much trouble to come by the boat. "How they had huffed and puffed", not to blow the house down, but to lift the boat up. It would appear that they intended to keep it in readiness until the moment that the order to abandon ship was given, being convinced that the moment must come.

Such action is in keeping with the maxim of this world: "I'm all right, Jack" and is at the farthest extremity from the golden rule and so called because it comprehends every beneficent principle enshrined in the 'Sermon on the Mount': "Therefore all things whatsoever ye would that men should do to you, do ye so even to them: for this is the law and the prophets"(Matt.7:12). A similar sentiment is voiced by the LORD in the aphorism: "He who seeks to save his life shall lose it: He who loses his life for My sake shall find it" (Matt.10:39). The charming story of the book of Ruth opens with an endorsement of that statement: "a famine in the land of Bethlehem" – meaning 'the House of Bread' – induced a man to sojourn in the land of Moab, which was as much out of bounds to an Israelite as the world is out of bounds for a Christian. It was only intended to be a temporary measure, but within a very short space of time, a premature death which he had tried to avoid overtook him in Moab. Ironically this man's name was Elimelech which means 'My God is King'. This was much at variance with his practice as he flouted the law of God. Within ten years both father and sons were dead (Ruth 1:3–5). Conversely, Ruth the young widow of Mahlon, went up from Moab to lose her life on Bethlehem's foreign soil as a companion to her mother-in-law Naomi, who had admitted she was bereft, desolate and indigent. To her old neighbours, who upon her return to the place of her birth greeted her by name, Naomi or 'Pleasant One', she lamented that her name given her at birth was now inappropriate. "I've changed it to Marah or bitterness for I went out full – of hope and expectation, and with a happy family – but the LORD hath brought me home again empty" (Ruth 1:21). Verily she was the prodigal daughter of Old Testament history.

Ruth had volunteered to lose her life by identifying with a desolate widow, to share a widow's poverty and eventually her grave; and swore to her asseveration with the most solemn vow that anyone could ever make. Her act of self-renunciation was an anticipation of Christ's call to discipleship, and earned herself a golden future, richer and fuller and more rewarding and enduring than anything she could have envisaged in her wildest dreams, and, to cap it all, eternal fame, (Ruth 4:13–15), all of which had been negated by her forecast implied in her expression of loyalty to her mother-in-law.

One of the greatest tributes ever paid to a body of Christians was that of Paul's to the believers of Macedonia: "Moreover, brethren, we do you to wit of the grace of God bestowed upon the churches of Macedonia; How that in a great trial of affliction the abundance of their joy and their deep poverty abounded unto the riches of their liberality … Praying us with much intreaty that we would receive the gift … And this they did, not as we had hoped, but first gave their own selves to the LORD, and unto us by the will of God" (2 Cor.8:1–5). It is impossible not to see the stark contrast between the grace of God evinced by the Macedonians and the graceless lives of the Egyptian seamen.

Jeremiah's picture of the deceitful heart is demonstrated vividly in the degrading action of the ship's crew, or as the time-worn dictum runs: "Every man for himself and the devil take the hindmost". His derogatory description of the unpredictable selfishness of man's heart was of it excelling everything else in artifice; its reputation was one of deceitfulness above all things. Even the most vicious of creatures are fairly predictable in their menacing actions: a lion gives warning of an imminent attack by threshing its tail. A missionary who had shot more than forty lions and thereby rendered yeoman services to villages menaced by the predators at night, was an authority on their habits and practices and categorically declared that when a lion swished its tail twice it was a signal that it was to leap upon its quarry. Before attacking, a snake gives warning by hissing, while a cobra extends its hood menacingly. Far from revealing an action of treachery, a man will do the opposite and feign an air of goodwill. These men in the story pretended to be concerned about the safety of all on board, but were about to ditch them, while using the lifeboat to make a getaway. So desperately wicked were they that they were ready to put at risk, and even sacrifice everyone else on board, as long as they saved themselves. God intimated that the depths of cupidity and infamy of a man's heart are beyond the scope of the lead to plumb, and asked the question "Who can know it?" and answers it Himself, for no one else, not even an angel can. "I the LORD search the heart, I try the reins, or the desires, to give to every man according to his ways" (Jer.17:9, 10).

Forty potential assassins planned to kill Paul by an artifice involving the chief priests and the council. Under the pretext of questioning Paul more concerning his Christian persuasions they were to appeal to the chief captain to bring him before them the next day, and they would ambush him and kill him. God, however, exposed the plot and Lysias the Roman Tribune, under a powerful armed escort, hurried him out of town and transported him to Cæsarea to Felix the Roman Governor that same night.

A sample of perfidy in its worst colour is that of Joab's cruel and dastardly subterfuge in engineering the death of one of his outstanding soldiers, Uriah the Hittite. In connivance with the king he arranged for the faithful and unsuspecting Uriah to be assigned to the most dangerous sector of the wall of Rabbah, which was under siege. At a given signal his comrades were to withdraw and leave Uriah to be exposed to the defending archers, so that he was a sitting-duck target for the volley of arrows that were fired at him, and under the fuselage he fell. David's sin with Bathsheba was cunningly concealed and Joab had secured the good books of the king. But David was soon to discover to his dismay that "God requireth that which is past".

Personal danger will bring out the selfishness of the human heart more than any other factor. Satan's no-holds-barred assault upon Job was preceded by a verbal barrage that encapsulated the slander: "All that a man hath will he give for his life" (Job 2:4). In short, Satan's slander inferred that the best of men, even a perfect man like Job, as complimented by God, will often prevaricate to save their own reputations, and, much more so, their own skins. For example, there was the treacherous action of the resident of Bethel who was captured by the men of Joseph, who were reconnoitring the city, with its capture in mind. They promised to spare his life if he would show them the secret entry in to the city. To this he acceded, and they took the city with the minimum of casualties and trouble and allowed the man his freedom. That the inhabitants were butchered caused him no remorse and lost him no sleep (Judges 1:22 –6). Where there is an absence of grace in the heart there will be none in the life.

Deceit and hypocrisy both come from the same stable of pretence or false colours. Hypocrisy is largely met with wearing a religious garb, but deceit is practised widely in secular affairs and relationships, but both belong to the realm of pretence. Herod was most convincing in religious colours. Most of his forty years as king were taken up with religious matters. Notably, his pride and joy was the building of the Temple. His superficiality is seen through, however, and is exposed in his rage at being snubbed by the wise men from the East who had come to worship a newborn babe, whom they had been supernaturally advised was the King of the Jews. Their enquiries as to the place of His birth came to Herod's ears. He expressed his desire to worship Him and invited them to report back and reveal His whereabouts. But God who knows the depths of depravity of the human heart warned them that Herod planned to destroy the Child and told them to return to their far-eastern home by another route and to do so with all speed. A man who will use religious ordinance or a pretentious act of worship to commit murder has no fear of God and will stop at nothing to foster his own evil designs, and knows no limit to his propagation of evil. When Herod was foiled in his murderous intention to destroy the child Jesus, he engineered a programme of mass child slaughter throughout the coasts of Bethlehem. Well aware that he was held in revulsion by the majority of his subjects; and that his death was impending, which would be an occasion of joyful celebration, he ordered that ten of Jerusalem's chief citizens were to be imprisoned and put to death as soon as his own death was announced. Few things more inhuman could ever have been devised. Providentially this ruthless order was not carried out; Herod's successors were a more humane body, and the captive citizens were released.

In abandoning what they assumed was a sinking ship, the mariners betrayed their scepticism in the apostle's confident assertion that there would be no loss of life, for God had, through his intercession and supplication, given him all those of the boat's crew and company who comprised his fellow voyagers. Paul's initial forecast of the tempestuous blast that would turn the sea into a maelstrom and precipitate the loss of cargo and ship when the prevailing weather conditions at the time of his prediction were good, should have convinced even the most incredulous that he was in possession of inside information, and had thereby proved that his information was from a divine and infallible source. Moreover, that it was their stubbornness and unbelief that had brought them to the brink of destruction.

Long before this Christ had laid great stress on the trustworthiness of the Scriptures, properly called the Bible, and enforced this truth upon the diehard signmongers by relating the story of the rich man who was in great torments in hell, while his erstwhile neighbour, a penurious and sore-ridden beggar, was being regaled by Abraham in Paradise. He so far forgot himself as to appeal to the patriarch to despatch Lazarus, the ex-beggar, to his family home to warn them of a future torment awaiting them unless they turned to God and repented, only to receive the answer, "They have Moses and the prophets. If they will not believe them, neither would they if one rose from the dead" (Luke 16:25–31). Later on in His ministry the LORD proved His point, when He raised a man of the same name: Lazarus the brother of the two godly sisters Martha and Mary, from the dead. Yet far from convincing His critics, it entrenched them more firmly in the prejudice of their crass non-belief. (John 12:9–11).

Only Paul's timely intervention had saved the travellers from a watery grave. Unbelief ever places more confidence in its prowess and ability to negotiate its own deliverance, and the shipmen were determined to shift for themselves, which bears out this premise. This attitude is characteristic of those whose faith is in what they can see. The believer's stance, however, is defined in *Hebrews* as those who are wholly convinced that "faith is the substance of things hoped for and the evidence of things not seen" (Heb.11:7). It says in the verse before "That him who comes to God must believe that He is and that He is a rewarder of them that diligently seek Him" (Heb.11:6) and further that without this quality of faith "it is impossible to please God".

How they had struggled to save the lifeboat from being battered and sunk was earlier related. Now the same people were struggling to refloat it and thereby get themselves safely to land, without a single thought for the welfare of the others on board. In spite of this, Paul's charge to the soldiers to restrain the sailors and prevent them leaving the ship in distress would conspire to the salvation of everyone.

From time immemorial men have pitted their unbelief and ability against the promises of God, and have just as often been confounded. In the history of the kings of Judah it is recorded how God had honoured King Asa by signal deliverances from overwhelming foreign invaders during his extended forty-one years of spectacular government. God had always given victory to his arms, when appealed to, but at the very last fence Asa faltered, and fell. King Asa, it is written, was diseased in his feet during the last two years of his reign: "And Asa in the thirty-ninth year of his reign was diseased in his feet until his disease was exceeding great: yet in his disease he sought not to the LORD but to the physicians. And Asa slept with his fathers, and died in the one and fortieth year of his reign" (2 Chron.16:12–13).

* * * * * * * * * * * * * * * * * * *

SERMON 18

DRASTIC ACTION: SALVATION BY ABIDING

Acts 27:31–32: *Paul said to the centurion and to the soldiers, Except these abide in the ship, ye cannot be saved. Then the soldiers cut off the ropes of the boat, and let her fall off.*

Paul in the providence of God had taken over the command of the ship. It had no binnacle nor lodestone, and no one on board with acumen enough to know what to do next, or whose orders and directions were trustworthy. A similar situation prevailed in Egypt – superpower though it were. The enigmatical dream given to Pharaoh had baffled the pundits which made up the circle of Egypt's intelligentsia. Joseph was called upon and brilliantly demonstrated his superior powers in the superb explanation of the twin dreams of Pharaoh, and without forethought or hesitation the subsequent counsel he gave as to the plan to adopt to best utilise the surplus grain of the seven years of successive bumper crops. Joseph's plan revealed a mind that was extraordinarily acute and perspicuous. Pharaoh instantly recognised in Joseph the only man who was sufficiently – nay, divinely – gifted to meet the current crisis, and as it were, knighted him on the spot, making him lord of all Egypt, before whom everyone was commanded, from the greatest to the least, to bow the knee, which truly bore out the proverb: "A man's gift maketh room for him and bringeth him before great men" (Prov.18:16).

God in His infallible judgement negotiated Paul's preferment and so exercised His God-given wisdom that all, from the captain and owner, not excluding the centurion, with all on board, had an

135

inward intuition that their salvation was in Paul's hands. In turn that innate witness was boosted by the conviction that they had survived up to that point through his prayers offered up for their sakes.

Nevertheless, the skill of the sailors was indispensable to their eventually landing on solid ground and achieving salvation. Only the sailors could reef a sail; handle the rudder, which comprised two paddles; and set the right sail to catch the prevailing wind that would blow them into the required harbour.

> One ship sails east, one ship sails west
> By the self-same wind that blows,
> It's not the way of the gales, but the set of the sails,
> That determines the way it goes.

Salvation involves the whole man, 'spirit, soul and body', "And the very God of peace sanctify you wholly; and I pray God your whole spirit and soul and body be preserved blameless unto the coming of our LORD Jesus Christ. Faithful is He that calleth you, who also will do it." (1 Thess.5:23–4). Under the heading of soul is comprehended reason, understanding, judgement, imagination and memory, which are known as the faculties of the mind, which plays an important part in a person's salvation and upon which the Bible places great emphasis. When asked by a Jewish lawyer what was the greatest commandment, Christ's explicit reply was, "Thou shalt love the LORD with all thine heart, with all thy soul, with all thy mind, and with all thy strength" (Matt.22:37; Luke10:26–8).

No man is at liberty to divorce his mind from the other entities of his tri-partite nature. In his rules for the Christian's spiritual warfare, Paul, as it were, legislated that "the weapons of our warfare are not carnal, but mighty through God to the casting down of strongholds, casting down imaginations and everything that exalteth itself against the knowledge of God, and bringing every thought into captivity to the obedience of Christ" (2 Cor.10:4–5), which being interpreted implies that "having surrendered the will, the faculties of the mind are given up to rendering to Christ the obedience of faith" (John Wesley). The Spirit of Christ or the Holy Spirit was never intended to be a substitute for the absence of brains in an empty cranium. God is served by the mind as well as the body. When the mind remains unsurrendered then there can be no salvation. It cannot be insulated from the remaining faculties in a Christian. There are no unsurrendered areas, for where such an incongruous state is extant, it is impossible that salvation can obtain. A dedicated heart means a surrendered will, and by logical assent, a dedicated whole. On this sound principle Paul, under the superintendence of God, wisely commanded the sailors to abide in the ship.

Christ taught the essential duty of abiding in Him, and, observing this relationship as a condition of salvation to those Jews who professed belief in Him, He articulates as their duty: "If ye continue in My Word, then, are ye My disciples indeed, and ye shall know the truth, and the truth shall make you free" (John 8:31–2). Only by putting into practice what they confessed would they enjoy true liberty – liberty of spirit – and deliverance from sin. As Ishmael the slave was expelled from the household of Abraham, so those who are the servants or bond slaves of sin will be ejected from the household of faith, "And the servant abideth not in the house for ever: but the Son abideth ever" (John 8:35), as will all who are made free from the guilt and power of sin by the Son, and become sons in consequence. Again the LORD said, "Abide in Me, and I in you. As the branch cannot bear fruit of itself, except it abide in the vine; no more can ye, except ye abide in Me" (John 15:4). Be sure of this: where there is no surrendered mind there can be no surrendered will. Araunah the ex-Jebusite king of Jebus, otherwise ancient Jerusalem, fully co-operated with David to placate the wrath of the judicial angel poised over Jerusalem with a naked sword, Araunah and his sons were threshing wheat with oxen on their threshing floor, but the angel required Araunah to offer those oxen on that very spot as a burnt offering to an outraged God. Araunah's magnanimous gesture to David is worthy to be emulated by all who would secure the favour of God. His spontaneous response to David was, "Take it to thee ... lo I give thee the oxen also for burnt offerings, and the threshing instruments for wood, and the wheat for a meat offering; I give it all" (1 Chron.21:23). Had one of those factors been withheld the sacrifice would have been defective and invalid, and the angel of retribution would have resumed the work of slaughter, instead of which the sword was resheathed.

Notice the dogmatic tone of the apostle's assertion: "ye cannot be saved", and addressed with authority to the Roman centurion, the man under orders to Cæsar. In effect the apostle was saying, "Ignore the charge and you will forfeit God's goodwill and saving ability", as was demonstrated by Jonah when he cried out in the whale's belly. "Salvation is of the LORD and the LORD spake unto the fish, and it vomited out Jonah upon the dry land" (Jonah 2:10).

Without quibbling, the soldiers' response was immediate, and they cut off the ropes of the boat, which fell into the sea. Their response to Paul's peremptory charge settled the matter of his final authority. He left no one under any illusion: "All of you will perish" and put "Except these abide in the ship, ye cannot be saved". Paul did not say "We cannot be saved". His safety had been guaranteed by God, who, as it were, had given Paul his ticket, for he had special business at the Court of Nero, in Rome, and included in the ticket were Luke and Aristarchus his fellow companions. All three carried the sanction of heaven. Only men of God dare speak with such confidence in the hearing of their social and professional superiors without appearing insolent, and not be excluded from their divinely given privileges.

It was a crucial situation and called for drastic action. Most certainly the soldiers and their commanding officer were inhibited by the magnitude of their danger which involved their own demise. Their reaction was one of swift decision. Coupled with the awe with which they had come to regard Paul, the decision to dispense with their boat, which was kept for emergencies, needed no further seconding.

In disposing of the boat so summarily, the apostle brings into the light of day the pettiness of our own foolish schemes. God doesn't need our puny boats to further His ends. Well might the Psalmist cross-examine the Jordan and ask, "What aileth thee O thou Jordan that thou wast driven back?" (Psalm 114:5), and the answer lay in the presence of the Ark of the Covenant, upon the shoulders of the priest, standing in the exposed bed of the river, that drove it back and exposed many miles of its bed, though in spate and having overflowed its banks, a mile or so on either side. "Driven back" was the best description of the retreating waters. In fact far beyond the city of Adam, which as it displays a wonder so it enshrines a truth, Christ the heavenly Ark of the Covenant, entered into the waters of the Jordan of death and eternal judgement, to drive them far back from the family of Adam "and to deliver those who through fear of death were all their lifetime subject to bondage" (Heb.2:10). "Christ", it is further written, "hath abolished death and brought life and immortality to light through the Gospel" (2 Tim.1:10). How many days must Israel have had to queue to transport their two million immigrants over the Red Sea, and how great a fleet of ships would have had to be commandeered! God negotiated the whole operation in one night, including herds of cattle and flocks of sheep, without a hoof being left behind.

Every Christian should be as adroit in using the knife as the Roman soldiers, or, better still, as Alexander the Greek conqueror, and of Gordian knot fame. This legendary knot was said to have been woven of rope made from the bark of a tree which Gordian used to fasten his yoke to a beam so ingeniously that no one could untie it. Legend had it that Alexander was told that whoever undid the knot would reign over the whole East. "Well then," said the conqueror, "it is thus that I perform the task", and so saying cut the rope in twain with his sword. Thus to cut the Gordian knot is to get out of a difficult position, by one's decisive step, to resolve a situation by force or by evasive action (*Brewer's Dictionary of Phrase and Fable*).

To use the knife often requires drastic action, as with Sir Wilfred Grenfell of Labrador fame. His means of transport as a missionary among the ice and frozen waste of Labrador was by dog team. While crossing a stretch of frozen sea on one of his mercy missions – he was a medical missionary – a section of the ice broke away, and he found himself being swept out to sea. His situation was precarious, but his immediate danger was that of exposure to Arctic temperatures, which would have been many degrees below zero. His parlous position called for immediate and drastic action. Taking out his knife he killed three of his dogs, and skinned them, putting their thick coats over his own clothes, after which he removed the flesh from the bones and fixed the bones in such a manner as to form a flagstaff, to which he attached a piece of white cloth dyed with the blood of his dogs, and so make it conspicuous against the white background of ice. In that position, marooned for some hours if not days, he waited patiently, if not anxiously. His patience was rewarded when a passing ship spotted him and rescued him. His salvation was his knife and probably a surgeon's scalpel. Under God it was the means of Wilfred Grenfell's salvation.

Sometimes the use of the knife is indicative of finality, meaning that it will now be impossible for a specific action to be repeated as the physical amputation has been so dramatic. Once a limb has been severed the die is cast. Christ's teaching concerning an offending eye or hand, or foot, was intended to enforce the gravity of a particular practice or action which demanded complete dissociation from it, as when amputating a part of the body. Normally such physical surgery is only performed to halt the spread of the poison or gangrenous condition to the rest of the body and precipitating the death of the individual. When the LORD commanded the removal of any part of the torso by using a knife, He never intended that it should be taken literally, no more than when He said, "Except ye eat the flesh of the Son of Man, and drink His blood, ye have no life in you" (John 6:53). Many, mistakenly, took Him literally and abandoned His cause. Had they waited they would have heard Him clarify His statement by a qualifying one: "It is the spirit that quickeneth; the flesh profiteth nothing: the words that I speak unto you, they are spirit and they are life" (John 6:63), in fine, grasp the inner and spiritual significance.

By the hand is to be understood as a habit or practice inconsistent with your holy calling, which hinders your spiritual growth or usefulness. Applying the Word of God to the stumbling practice which discloses its evil is tantamount to dispelling it. Some Christians have developed a conscience about time-consuming television watching or the eulogising of lust, which deliberately promotes evil, and have terminated their licences or scrapped their sets, which is tantamount to cutting off the soul-destroying passion. Their eyes offend them by what they see and consequently operate upon the offending member, and, as it were, pluck it out. When Manasseh rid Jerusalem of the idols which he had introduced, the action was superficial. Instead of burning them he simply threw them out of the city, so that upon his death, Amon his son retrieved them and placed them on their pedestals (2 Chron.33:15, 22).

A knife is an instrument that makes a clean cut when well honed, and for that reason God commanded Joshua to take sharp knives and circumcise all the males in Israel, as soon as they had crossed the Jordan and encamped at Gilgal. A sharp knife ensured a clean and not a jagged cut, for the ordinance displayed their clean severance from Egypt, as a preparation for their entry into Canaan, where everything pertaining to Egypt 'the Land of Bondage', was prohibited in 'the Land of Promise'. Baptism is the

New Testament counterpart of circumcision, and explains why Peter commanded the people "to repent and be baptised in the name of Jesus Christ for the remission of sins" … and exhorted them, saying, "Save yourselves from this untoward generation" (Acts 2:38, 40). For the execution of this duty there is no knife or sword sharper than the Word of God, which is defined as "quick and powerful and sharper than any two-edged sword, piercing even to the dividing asunder of soul and spirit, and of the joints and marrow, and is a discerner of the thoughts and intents of the heart" (Heb.4:12). Through the agency of that sword or knife a truly circumcised Christian has divorced himself from the world, with its medley of practices, diversions, schemes and pleasures, never to return to them. The knife of God's Word will have disposed of them so cleanly, as if they had never been.

In the list of Temple vessels drawn up by Ezra, which were restored by Ezra and brought back to Jerusalem, there were named twenty-nine knives, which were sandwiched between thirty chargers of gold and thirty basins of gold (Ezra 1:9–10). Reading between the lines, and much Bible truth is featured between the lines, it may be logically concluded that there was a lost or missing knife, for thirty is twice mentioned when naming the chargers and basins. Speaking figuratively, to lose a knife in its spiritual context is not unusual. Moses mislaid the knife of circumcision for forty years and made no attempt to find it. Abraham's determination to sacrifice Isaac in response to God's command on Mount Moriah was evinced by his taking the knife. As it happened, however, God provided a substitute in the shape of a ram caught in a thicket, and the knife was used on the ram's throat and not on Isaac's.

A story is related of an Alpiner who used his knife to sever the rope of the comrade to whom he was tethered. This comrade had slipped and was left dangling over the edge of an ice crevasse. The Alpiner did not have enough strength to pull him back to safety and so to save himself being dragged over by the weight of his fallen comrade, he cut the rope sending the man to his death. Days later, when the body was recovered, the truth came out as a decisive, clean cut in the cross-section of the rope betrayed that it had been a deliberate act.

Times there are when we must part with all other help before we can expect God's interposition, that He might have all the credit. Like Ruth, we must be past all other help, and our confidence must be in Christ, our heavenly Boaz, alone. In that pastoral story the nearer kinsman to Ruth had no power to redeem an outcast Moabite young woman, so Boaz stepped in and filled the breach. Parallel to that story is the story of Christ, the heavenly Boaz, who has stepped in to do what the nearer Kinsman, called the law, had no ability to do, that is to redeem self-confessed sinners. "For what the law could not do, in that it was weak through the flesh, God sending His own Son in the likeness of sinful flesh, and for sin, condemned sin in the flesh: That the righteousness of the law might be fulfilled in us, who walk not after the flesh, but after the Spirit" (Rom.8:3–4). Christ intervened and answered all the legal demands of the law of God and by His death purchased beggared sinners like Ruth the Moabitess to be His heavenly bride (Ruth 4:5–10).

It was painfully evident there was no room for a shipload of people in the small boat, no more than the Law of God has space or place or grace for a shipload of sinners. When Christ hung on the cross, in His circumcision we were circumcised, and have put off the body of the sins of the flesh, not made with hands, but by the operation of God, inwardly wrought (Col.2:11–12). "Salvation must ever be of the LORD" (Jonah 2:9).

* * * * * * * * * * * * * * * * * * * *

SERMON 19

THE APPROACHING DAY OF SALVATION

Acts 27:33–6: *While the day was coming on.*

At this juncture the ship is very near land and the day is about to break. For all on board it is the day of their salvation. Paul's concern is that they be prepared for it, which was not a little like Moses – Paul's Old Testament counterpart – on the eve of Israel's departure from the land of Egypt, the country of their bondage. Israel's readiness necessitated the taking of a last meal on Egyptian soil – the Passover meal of the roast Passover lamb. While eating they were commanded to be shod, not slippered, grasping their staves and in a standing position. At break of day they had to be on their way, which would give them no time to knead their dough, but it was to be wrapped in their clothes and carried on their shoulders in the kneading troughs. The whole exercise was to be performed in haste, before Pharaoh changed his mind and revoked his decision to leave Israel and go.

A not dissimilar situation prevailed with the vessel and ship's company. The storm still raged and the wind was howling. Within a very little the night would have given way to early morning, which would spell their only opportunity of making land safely. That opportunity had to be grasped with both hands: it was then or never.

Paul in his letter to the Romans used an expression that summed up their predicament. His remark was, "The night is far spent, the day is at hand, let us therefore cast off the works of darkness, and let us put on the armour of light" (Rom.13:12). An able Bible expositor has likened "this life to a night, the resurrection to the day; the Gospel shining on the heart to the dawn of the day". We are charged "to awake out of sleep and throw away our nightclothes, and put on new (our day wear). The day dawns when we receive faith and then sleep gives place".

Earnestly, therefore, the apostle exhorted them to take food and end a long fast, having eaten nothing for fourteen days. How concerned the disciples had been because the multitude had been with them for three days, during which period they had been without food and had earnestly appealed to the LORD to send them home, lest any of them faint by the way. For the second time the fourteenth day is mentioned and, as pointed out in an earlier sermon, would seem to equate to that period which terminates uncertainty and lack of assurance. During their season on board "all hope that they should be saved had been taken away". The fear of death, like the sword of Damocles hanging over their heads, had robbed them of all desire for food, and sleep was out of the question. "Let us not wonder then, if men who have a deep sense of everlasting death, for a time forget to eat their bread or to attend their worldly affairs. Much less, let us not censure that as madness which may be the beginning of true wisdom" (John Wesley). Labouring under a deep sense of conviction and kicking against the goads of an outraged conscience, Saul of Tarsus neither ate nor drank for three days, but, totally blind, wrestled with his guilt for three days in the house of one Judas, in the street called 'Straight' (Acts 9:9). John Nelson, one of Wesley's outstanding travelling preachers, a man of benign and God-fearing character, was smitten with such a sense of sin and undoneness after hearing Wesley preach on Kensington Common, that the sight of food became loathsome to him, and eat he could not, which reduced him to such a strait that his gracious landlady and her husband told him that he must leave their house, for they feared he was losing his reason. On the day that he called to clear his debts and collect his clothes, they changed their mind, and said they would not let him leave. Unknown to them John Nelson had desperately prayed and the LORD had answered by changing their minds. Such was the answer which for abruptness could hardly have been more abridged. Nelson said, like a drowning man catching at a straw, "Save or damn!" and immediately he was given by the Spirit of God the full assurance of forgiveness and salvation.

Matthew's genealogy table of the ancestors of Christ is made up of forty-two generations, from Abraham to Christ, and that in turn is broken up into three periods of fourteen generations. Forty-two has been defined as dispensational completeness of evil. It is written in the Revelation that the Beast emerged from the sea and, envenomed by the dragon, alias Satan, was empowered by the wicked one to devastate the earth and blaspheme God, which power was given to him to continue forty-two months, during which time he made war with the saints and overcame them (Rev.13:4 –7), but when he flexed his military muscles and satanic might against the all-conquering Son of God, he was without ceremony removed from the head of his vast army and cast into the Lake of Fire (Rev.19:11–16; Rev.19:19–20).

Each period ended an unsatisfactory dispensation: the patriarchal, the regnant, and that of vassalage; and all rounded off by the advent of Christ, the anointed Saviour and Deliverer (Matt.1:1–17), by which the promised seed to Abraham was fulfilled.

Paul had confidently predicted that they would be all saved. Notwithstanding, they were waiting with not a little apprehension for the arrival of that day, which was virtually about to break. There is a strong correspondence between their uncertainty and that of the women who set out while it was dark, bearing spices that they had painstakingly prepared during the period of Christ's entombment. A problem weighed on their minds concerning the stone, and discussing it as they made their way, they asked each other, "Who shall roll us away the stone from the door of the sepulchre?" Upon their arrival, the sun had arisen, by the light of which they saw their problem was illusionary. The stone had been moved from the entrance of the sepulchre (Mark 16:1–2; John 20:1). Their arrival would have coincided with the sunrise, which in turn would have been the identical moment that Christ the Sun of Righteousness had risen from the dead, which too was coincidental with the removal of the stone: not three distinct times but together simultaneously. During the darkness of our nights of unbelief our problems seem insurmountable; when Christ arises and shines upon us, they have been removed. The Psalmist could not have worded it better than when he remarked, "They looked unto Him and were lightened and their faces were not ashamed" or "their faces were radiant" (Psalm 34:5).

To ensure that the day of their salvation should be a reality and not a fiasco it was essential that Paul's fellow travellers fortified themselves with nourishment. Paul consequently behoved them, in his customary thoughtfulness, "I pray you take some meat for this is for your health." In the Hebrew language, salvation and health are interchangeable, which is brought out in Psalm 67:2, where it talks about "God's saving health among all nations". Likewise, without God's nourishment instinct in His Word there can be no soul health or salvation. Strong faith spells spiritual health. Psalm 104:15 speaks of "bread which strengtheneth man's heart". Faith is derived from the Word of God and is spoken of "as the word of faith, which we preach" (Rom.10:8), and in the same setting it asserts, "So then faith cometh by hearing and hearing by the Word of God" (Rom.10:17). It is this faith, therefore, which is begotten by "the receipt of perceived truth", which engenders the grace of salvation as presented by Titus: "For the grace of God that bringeth salvation hath appeared to all men" (Titus 2:11) and perhaps the most conclusive of all the Scriptures concerning the efficacy of grace is repeated in the second chapter of the letter to the Ephesians: "For by grace ye are saved through faith, and that not of yourselves, it is the gift of God" (Ephes.2:5, 8). Luke notes the glaring discrepancy between the Jews of Thessalonica and those of Berea. Of the latter the writer pays the fulsome compliment of being more noble than the former and subjoins the reason that "they received the Word" which Paul preached to them, "with all readiness of mind, and searched the Scriptures daily whether those things were so. Therefore many of them believed" (Acts 17:1:10–13). As for the non-believing element in Thessalonica, "they set in the city in an uproar" (Acts 17:5). It cannot be gainsaid that the Word of God is the cardinal factor in men's salvation. Paul's promise to all on board the doomed ship was one of complete salvation, and he drove it home in words meant to be taken literally and not hyperbolically: "Not a hair shall fall from the head of any of you", which is all the more astounding by virtue of their being between seventy to a hundred thousand hairs on the human head. In Bible typology the hair of the head is an emblem of consecration, as indicated in the Nazarite vow, which required that a Nazarite, which means 'separated one', must never submit to his head being shorn or shaven (Numbers 6:5). It was the violation of this ordinance that led to the disastrous downfall of Samson. Not a hair of their head falling is a highly figurative way of saying that their salvation would be a full salvation. Speaking of the superlative ministry of Christ, who is called "the High Priest after the order of Melchisedec", the writer affirms, "Wherefore He is able to save them to the uttermost, or completely, that come unto God by Him" (Heb.7:25).

Paul was not only proving to all that he was the only master mariner on board that vessel, but he was the only person present fully assured of his ultimate appointment with Cæsar. In the reckoning of God he was already home and dry, and in God's good time, not the emperor's time, would be conducting his own brief before Nero. Paul's immediate concern was for his fellow voyagers, and because the bent of his being was the salvation of men, "He became all things to all men that he might save some" (1 Cor.9:19–22), and succinctly expressed the leading temper of his soul.

In urging them to get ready for the final leg of their turbulent journey, Paul used a word of urgency that he had used when appealing to the Corinthians as one whose status was that of an ambassador for Christ.

An ambassador is one who is sent by a sovereign or by one state to another state. Paul's language is significant; he appealed to them "as though God did beseech you by us, we pray you in Christ's stead be ye reconciled to God" (2 Cor.5:19–20), "and hath committed unto us the word of reconciliation" (verse 19). Using the same word and displaying the same gentle spirit he appealed to the shipload of storm-battered passengers and mariners, who were hanging on his every word as their one hope and confidence. "He besought them to take some meat" or "he prayed them" whereupon he demonstrated his full confidence in the faithfulness and ability in the God he had already borne testimony to of His making good His promise. He took bread before them all and after giving thanks to God and breaking it he began to eat, just as he had done many times in the Breaking of Bread services in the churches he had pioneered through his able ministry. It was an ordinary meal but he transposed it into a memorial service of the Body of Christ, which had been broken for the sins of the whole world.

Unashamedly Paul gave thanks to God in the company of them all: Egyptian idolaters, pagan Romans, coarse seamen and superior heathens. Men of God are overawed in no company for such a one constantly stood in awe of the great God and Saviour Jesus Christ, "who only hath immortality dwelling in the light which no man can approach unto" (1 Tim.6:16). He followed out to the letter the dictum of David: "Stand in awe and sin not" (Psalm 4:4). And those who so reverence God fear not the great nor flatter the wealthy; neither do they cringe before the baser sort of a depraved society. Julian the centurion observed at close quarters that Paul was no court flunkey, and had not been cowed by the star-studded auditory that were present when he set forth his case before King Agrippa.

Paul's dumbstruck audience must have wondered why anyone should bother to give thanks for bread, which is, after all, the lowest common denominator in the food line, when beneath their feet was a shipload of grain that would never be milled or grace a bakery. The truth was he must needs emulate His gracious Master, the LORD Jesus, who had given thanks for bread to His heavenly Father, which His own disciples had disdained, saying, "What are these among so many?" and by doing so, He had made a place famous by His imprecatory effusion and immortalised it by His giving thanks to God (John 6:23).

"Then were they all of good cheer." The simplest exercise that honours God can have widespread repercussions for good. A young girl's ecstatic testimony in a prayer meeting in Wales sparked off the Welsh revival. Spontaneously she rose from her seat in the church and with great emotion said, "O I do love Jesus!" and that simple but earnest statement was the spark to the tinder.

Paul's carriage of cheerfulness spread rapidly, for real joy is infectious. Very much was this the case with Sarah at the birth of Isaac: she was induced by Abraham to call him Isaac, meaning laughter, and accompanied it with a word of explanation, saying, "God hath made me to laugh, so that all that hear me will laugh with me" (Gen.21:6), for few things are more contagious.

Theirs was the joy of anticipation and more so because of the extensive period of fear and misery. Paul's joy was innate and whose reality is intimated in the proverb: "The heart knoweth his own bitterness, and a stranger doth not intermeddle with his joy" (Prov.14:10). And in this respect the apostle was a true Benjamite – literally 'a son of the right hand' or 'a son of joy' – for at God's right hand there are pleasures for evermore. Rachel would have perpetuated her misery and christened him Ben-oni – 'son of sorrow' – but in spite of his own sorrow, Jacob quashed it and changed the name to Benjamin, 'a son of the right hand' or 'son of joy'. Paul's joy was not sporadic but experiential, which was confirmed by his praises in the gaol at Philippi, that so fascinated the inmates. His joy was his strength and his forte, and consequently encouraged them while his faith had inspired them.

Paul's heavenly carriage in the vortex of a storm had brought heaven down to them. "They were all of good cheer, and took some meat". It was that simple repast that was their salvation. A compassionate apostle was much concerned. Not only were they physically debilitated because of their protracted fast, but were suffering from hypothermia. Their bodies were below body temperature. In a matter of hours or even less they would be plunged into the cold waters of the Mediterranean. That they generate heat and energy was their immediate need. A hurried meal would quickly supply what was lacking.

Peter rounded off his maiden address to his large Jewish congregation most fittingly when he brought his speech to a climax with a powerful appeal. They were pricked in their hearts and said, "Men and brethren, what shall we do?" (verse 37), a question that was answered with: "Know assuredly that God hath made this same Jesus whom ye have crucified both LORD and Christ, repent and be baptised every one of you in the name of Jesus Christ for the remission of sins ... for the promise is unto you and your children ... and with many other words did he testify and exhort, saying, 'Save yourselves from this untoward generation'. Then they that gladly received his word were baptised, and the same day were added unto them about three thousand souls" (Acts 2:33–41).

And just as the ship's crew and company were all of good cheer and did take some meat, so the agitated hearers gladly received Peter's spiritual food and were inwardly nourished and fortified to save themselves from the waters of a greater flood than that which engulfed the world in Noah's day, namely the waters of divine judgement. Not for nothing has it been written, "His judgements are a great deep".

God's Word was likened in the writings of *Jeremiah* to a hammer that breaketh the rock as well as to a fire. "Is not My

Word like as a fire?" saith the LORD (Jer.23:29). On the day of the resurrection of Christ, Cleopas and a partner, when journeying to Emmaus from Jerusalem, were joined by a third party who treated them to an exhaustive exposition of the Scriptures from Moses to Malachi, and His topic was "Christ in all the Scriptures" (Luke 24:27). But it was only when He momentarily revealed His identity and vanished that they expressed the wonder of their experience: "Did not our hearts burn within us while He talked with us by the way and opened up the Scriptures?" (Luke 24:32) Not only were they heartwarmed but also fortified, and left uneaten their prepared evening meal, but with renewed strength returned to Jerusalem in great haste (verse 33).

"They took some meat", that is they ate the meat that was proffered them, and assimilated it. Only when the Word of God is imbibed does it become faith, which buttresses the heart and equips it for action. Until that is done, although very near and not far from the kingdom, salvation is still wishful thinking.

* * * * * * * * * * * * * * * * * * * *

SERMON 20

THE SHIP'S MUSTER ROLL

Acts 27:37: *And we were in all in the ship two hundred threescore and sixteen souls.*

Common prudence directed them to take a tally of all on board so that they could check the number of survivors against the original census, and satisfy themselves there were none missing in the final encounter with the boisterous sea. Paul's confident assertion was not only would there be no losses, but not a hair of their heads would perish. Amongst the seamen, whose plot of a clandestine escape had been foiled by Paul's disclosure, there probably would have been some who could have hoped that the apostle would be proved wrong. Had any of them worn wigs the promise would not have applied. Only genuine hair could expect to survive, as being covered by the promise of God, no more than the ropes with which the three Hebrew youths were bound before being cast into Nebuchadnezzar's furnace could have hoped to survive the flames, and he expressed his astonishment in this matter: "Did not I cast three men bound into the furnace, and lo I see four men loose walking in the midst of the fire, and they have no hurt; and the form of the fourth is like the Son of God" (Dan.3:23– 5). "God's promises are yea and amen in Christ Jesus" (2 Cor.1:20), and are open to the closest and most critical scrutiny.

Whether Paul was aware of the full complement of passengers and state prisoners and ship's personnel who boarded the Alexandrian grain ship at Myra bound for Italy cannot be determined, but his marathon session of prayer and agenda included them all, which is made clear by the wording of the angel's communication, which assured the apostle that his prayer had been heard, the drift of which was: "Lo God hath given thee all them that sail with thee" (Acts 27:23–4). And as there were two hundred threescore and sixteen souls on board the ship when they loosed from Myra, then the same number would be spared a watery grave, and by implication a fiery lake or hell. Paul's concern always reached far beyond the natural and the physical, which sentiment he alluded to in his final words to Timothy in the last letter that was ever dictated by the apostle. In that missive he deplored the faithlessness of the brethren, who took fright and abandoned him when he appeared before Cæsar. In spite, however, of their perfidy, he stressed that "God stood with him and strengthened him, that by him the preaching might be fully known, that all the Gentiles might hear" (2 Tim.4:17). It is hardly possible not to notice the similarity between Christ's letter and and the apostle's. Of Christ, is it said, "And they all forsook Him and fled" (Mark 14:50), but whereas Paul avers that "The LORD stood by him, and strengthened him, and delivered him out of the mouth of the lion" that is Satan, no such sequel was that of the LORD's, who cried out pathetically, "My God, My God, why hast Thou forsaken Me?" (Mark 15:34), and He was not delivered out of the mouth of the lion, but prayed, "Father into Thy hands I commend My spirit" (Luke 23:46), and as positively as Jonah was swallowed by the whale, so Christ was swallowed by death. "Now that He that ascended what is it but that He also descended first into the lower parts of the earth?" (Ephes.4:9)

That Paul had asked for all them that sailed with him was characteristic of the apostle's entire disposition, and must certainly have included their souls. It is quite unthinkable that he would have passed over their eternal state. Paul's calling was primarily the salvation of the souls of men. This was stressed in his appearance before Agrippa, to whom he unequivocally confessed that Christ, when He appeared to him, had given him his marching orders to "go to the Gentiles, to open their eyes, and to turn them from darkness to light and from the power of Satan unto God, that they might receive forgiveness of sins, and inheritance among them which are sanctified by faith that is in Me" (Acts 26:18), "Whereupon O King Agrippa, I was not disobedient to the heavenly vision" (Acts 26:19).

Two hundred threescore and sixteen souls is not an arbitrary figure, nor is it one that has been drawn out of a hat, but a number that like many other expressions and episodes in the Scriptures when compared show their connection of parts and serve to demonstrate its divine inspiration. Incidents which in other ways are quite unrelated have a common denominator which unites them although they may be historically separated by thousands of years. An excellent example is found in the divine directive concerning Israel's Exodus from Egypt, under the leadership of Moses the Lawgiver.

When the Lord spared the firstborn of all males of the families of the Hebrews from the general slaughter of the eldest sons of all Egyptian households, He claimed them as His, saying, "Sanctify unto Me all the firstborn, whatsoever openeth the womb among the Children of Israel, both of man and of beast, is Mine". Consequently He commanded that "all the firstborn of the children of Israel thou shalt redeem", which was enlarged upon later in the wilderness pilgrimage.

At Mount Sinai God gave notice of the building of a Tabernacle, which was to be the centre of their worship. The complicated ceremonial and ritual involved in that worship was to be carried out by a priesthood drawn from the males of the tribe of Levi and expressly from the family of Aaron and his descendants, and often spoken of as "the priesthood after the pattern of Aaron". The Levites' immediate function was the transporting of the Tabernacle and its furniture in their movements from one station to another during their journey from Egypt to Canaan, which comprised forty-two stations in all. Each station found their period of stay either longer or shorter according to the purpose of

God, but altogether spread out over a period of forty years.

Instead, however, of all the firstborn of all the families of the twelve tribes performing the sacred service, God exchanged the promiscuous firstborn males from all the tribes for all the males of the tribe of Levi. God's choice of Levi in preference to any of the other of the sons of Jacob was because of their proven devotion and faithfulness to Him during a time of crisis, which found the other tribes in serious default. Moses had been absent from the camp for forty days after his being summoned by God to the glory-crowned peak of Mount Sinai, to receive the Ten Commandments, and it was in the absence of Moses that the people agitated for a visible form of worship in the form of a calf, which was observed in Egpyt. Aaron was intimidated and weakly gave in to the agitators. Upon his return to base, as it were, Moses, to his dismay, found the majority of the people naked and dancing around the golden effigy. Levi alone had kept aloof, thus his appeal to all who were on the LORD's side, to gird on their swords and go through the camp from one gate to another and slaughter those who by their naked state and other outward signs had given themselves to idol worship. Levi immediately responded. None were to be spared on the grounds of consanguinity or sentiment. And in obeying the injunction of Moses, were acknowledged as having consecrated themselves to the LORD. Three thousand were slain that day by the Levites faithful to God, who had, as it were, sacrificed their brother to the LORD, where they had been guilty.

Altogether there were twenty-two thousand Levites (Numbers 3:39), while the firstborn of all other tribes were twenty-two thousand two hundred and seventy-three, which meant there were two hundred and seventy-three more of the firstborn of the other tribes than there were Levites. God decreed, therefore, that the overplus of two hundred and seventy-three were to be redeemed with silver. Each individual was to be redeemed at a ransom price of five shekels, with an explanatory statement that each shekel was equivalent to twenty gerahs, which made the redemption price equivalent to one hundred gerahs. In Bible numerology the figure of one hundred is an emblem of fullness.

Boaz's invitation to Ruth was to abide fast by his maidens, and to go after them wherever they went to reap. In addition she was invited to drink of that which his young men had drawn. They had been charged not to harm her in any way. Naturally his kindness quite overcame her and she fell down before him, overcome by his kindness, and enquired as to the reason of his gracious action, and an answer was immediately forthcoming. Boaz said to her, "It hath fully been shewed me, all that thou hast done unto thy mother-in-law since the death of thine husband: and how thou hast left thy father and thy mother, and the land of thy nativity, and art come unto a people which thou knewest not. Heretofore, the Lord recompense thy work, and a full reward be given thee of the Lord God of Israel, under whose wings thou art come to trust" (Ruth 2:11–12). Christ said, "There is no man who hath left father, mother, children, lands for My sake and the Gospel's who shall not receive an hundredfold in this world and in the world to come life everlasting" (Matt.19:29–30). Ruth had anticipated the promise a thousand years before it had been aired by the Lord.

Peter reminded his fellow Jews, whom he called strangers scattered among the nations, "Forasmuch as ye know that ye were not redeemed with corruptible things, as silver and gold, from your vain conversation received by tradition from your fathers; But with the precious blood of Christ, as of a lamb who verily was without blemish and without spot" (1 Peter 1:18–20). Paul's argument, which is appropriate to the background of a ship in distress, bound for Italy with a large contingent of Romans on board, and writing to the Roman believers, "For all have sinned, and come short of the glory of God; Being justified freely by His grace through the redemption that is in Christ Jesus: Whom God hath set forth to be a propitiation through faith in His blood, to declare His righteousness" (Rom.3:23–5). And again the apostle affirms, "To the praise of the glory of His grace, wherein He hath made us accepted in the beloved. In whom we have redemption through His blood, the forgiveness of sins, according to the riches of His grace" (Ephes.1:6–7).

Paul had asked God for all the souls that sailed with him, obviously meaning their lives, but knowing his awareness of the special grace dispensed to him for the salvation of immortal souls from eternal perdition, his intercession would not only have included a spiritual deliverance but it would have bulked large. Well might Paul have cried out, "Woe is me if I preach not the Gospel" had the main thrust of his intercessions and supplications been only for the bodily and natural requirements of humanity. It will be readily, and without presumption, admitted that on the grounds of Christ's universal redemption the full salvation of those souls would have been given him. And as their stay on the island on which they were soon to be cast would be for a period of some months, he would improve the occasion by nurturing them with the good Word of God.

It may be asked how can the two figures be reconciled seeing there is a disparity of three digits between the figure in the book of *Numbers* of two hundred and seventy-three, and that of the number comprising the ship's crew and company in the historical account given in the *Acts of the Apostles* of two hundred three-score and sixteen. It can be positively asserted that Paul would not have been praying for himself. Twice God had told him to "be of good cheer" (Acts 23:11), and to "fear not" (Acts 27:24), "for thou must appear before Cæsar". His life, therefore, was never in any danger. Nor would he have been praying for Aristarchus or Luke, who were his companions in travel and who would share his imprisonment in Rome. Luke, in his account of Paul's setting out for Rome, mentions that Aristarchus was with them. Writing his final letter to Timothy, Paul remarked that "only Luke is with me" (2 Tim.4:11) and passes over any reference to Aristarchus, who could well have died for it was several years after his arrival in the capital city of Rome that his final letter was written. In the

Colossian letter Aristarchus is cited again as his fellow prisoner, (Col.4:10), which was one of his several prison epistles (Col.4:18).

Three on board the grain ship were all Christians of repute and well seasoned in the faith, which reduced the number to two hundred and seventy-three for whom Paul would have offered impassioned and effectual prayer; and prayer that was all-embracing, inclusive of bodies and of their souls.

* *

SERMON 21

THE FINAL PREPARATIONS

Acts 27:38: *And when they had eaten enough, they lightened the ship, and cast out the wheat into the sea.*

It was important that they be shipshape and Bristol fashion. Their final leg was the most crucial, in which it would be a question of make or break. Actually, in their case, it would turn out to be make *and* break.

"When they had eaten enough" is suggestive of a disciplined appetite and although only a dry ship's biscuit, their hunger gave piquancy to the simple meal, for it has been aptly said that appetite is the best sauce. Paul, long before this voyage to Rome, had reminded his Corinthian readers that "he that striveth for masteries is temperate in all things", and qualified it by his own abstemiousness, claiming, "I keep under my body and bring it into subjection lest by any means when I have preached to others I myself should be a castaway" (1 Cor.9:25–7). They would soon be cast up, but were to do all in their power, for God would supplement their labour by performing that which was beyond their power, to avoid their being castaways.

So they wisely took Paul's advice and copied his example and ate of the available viands. Energy would be needful to tide them over the angry billows when they would address themselves to mastering the elements, in their final throes. Eat, therefore, they must. Significantly they did not gorge, but ate only what was sufficient; a terse statement indeed, but instinct with meaning.

John Bunyan in his brilliant and detailed exposition of Solomon's Temple, draws attention to the bellies of the two brazen pillars which stood like sentinels before the main doorway. Of those protuberances called the bellies, he commented that the belly is a craving thing, which demands that it be controlled, lest it controls the individual, which was the case with a large body within the Philippian assembly, of whom Paul wrote, "For many walk of whom I have told you often … whose god is their belly … who mind earthly things" (Phil.3:18–19). The bellies of the Temple pillars craved for the pomegranates festooned around the capitals and were hanging before them, representing the fruits and gifts of the Spirit which believers are charged to covet after: "Wherefore covet after charity and desire or covet – earnestly the best gifts" (1 Cor.12:31; 14:1).

To overindulge the physical appetite leads to debilitating the appetite of the inner or spiritual man, of which Solomon is a paramount example. Although the wisest person living he played the fool, of whom it is written, "King Solomon loved many strange women, and it came to pass, when Solomon was old, that his wives turned away his heart after other gods" (1 Kings 11:1, 4). He had indulged his bodily appetite to such an extraordinary degree that it momentarily eclipsed his love for God.

Eglon, King of Moab, whose name spells fat-tail, was disgustingly obese, as was King Henry VIII, whose philanderings are well aired in the history of his reign, and who became so portly that he required a carriage to support his corporation. Moab means 'a father' or 'of Adam', whose coveting of the fruit of 'the Tree of Knowledge of Good and Evil' introduced the principle of sin and the element of sin and death into the world (Rom.5:12). Eglon was the epitome of overindulgent flesh. Ehud, however, produced the answer, which was a dagger measuring a cubit in length, that is eighteen inches, and was an emblem of the Word of God and is described as sharp and two-edged (Heb.4:12). This he thrust into the protruding stomach of the Moabitish tyrant, the haft included, and repulsively observed that the dirt came out, which could be representative only of "filthiness of the flesh and of the spirit", long accumulated by protracted indulgence. In Ehud's radical action is a pregnant lesson, "They that are Christ's have crucified the flesh with the affections and lusts" (Gal.5:24).

When the prospective escapees on board the threatened Egyptian grain ship "had eaten enough" then "they lightened the ship". On the very eve of the Welsh revival, Evan Roberts was taking tea with a group of dedicated Christians in a home at Castle Emlyn or Lougher. He was proffered a plate of bread and butter towards the end of the meal, but graciously refused another slice, and used a fascinating expression, viz. "I am surfeited". When we have been surfeited with the things of this world, perhaps we may find ourselves on the threshold of revival. At this present time many of the LORD's people are much too enamoured by worldly things.

At the conclusion of the meal it was deemed necessary to lighten the ship and purge it of everything that was disposable that could impede their dash to the shore. A parallel might be drawn from the purging of all Jewish homes of leaven, which is fermented dough and a type of corruption or sin, on the day before the Passover celebration. On that day, known as the Day of Preparation, every room in the house was carefully searched for any leavened bread. Tables were scrubbed as well as floors. Nothing was left to chance. Paul draws an analogy between the Jewish Passover and the life of holiness demanded of a Christian. To default on the smallest sin is to corrupt the whole lump, and stresses that "a little leaven leaveneth the whole lump". One tolerated sin or sinful practice unfits one for heaven. His charge was unequivocal: "Purge out therefore the old leaven, that ye may be a new lump. For even Christ our Passover is slain for us". We are made holy through the slaying of Christ, the true Passover Lamb. The old leaven is to be purged, with that of malice, which is active ill will or wickedness, and the Feast kept with the unleavened bread of sincerity and truth, which is true holiness.

Twice before they had been exercised in riding out the tempest by disgorging all the superfluous ballast. This would be their last chance of descrying any overlooked hindrance to their survival. Runners are in the same boat, and the apostle uses the athlete who is aiming for gold as a stalking horse for those who are heavenward bound to "Lay aside every weight" – and all sins are weights which encumber the spirit. He likewise speaks of "the sin which so easily besets us" (Heb.12:1), or literally, the sin of our heels, which dogs us. A yelping, snapping dog will cause a runner to stop. John Nelson recorded in his journal that on journeying on foot to a distant preaching appointment, a journey which took him a number of hours, he was followed for miles by a mad dog, and that only the providence of God saved him from rabies and an awful death by hydrophobia.

On the second day of the tempest they lightened the ship, which involved casting overboard everything that could be dispensed with, yet without suffering any serious loss. When the third day brought no let-up of the storm, it was a matter of all hands on deck, with the prisoners being pressed into assisting in casting overboard the tackling of the ship with other heavy gear. Still there was no improvement in the erratic and destabilised motion of the ship. They despaired and gave themselves up for lost.

Nevertheless, after fourteen days the prayers and cheering words of the apostle had changed a grim situation into a hopeful one; a glimmer of light or hope could be seen at the end of the tunnel. And because of the radically changed situation, they resolved to go over the ship with a toothcomb to improve its chances of grounding on solid land by dispensing with any over-looked impediment, which really is an illustration of diligence, to which the Christian is frequently exhorted, and is nothing short of making a matter one's whole concern.

So great was the tempest buffeting the ship on which Jonah had booked a passage to take him to Tarshish, that the Scripture says, "The ship was like to be broken". Likewise an equably great fear possessed the mariners that they cast out the wares, while calling upon their gods. In desperation they cast lots, which indicated that Jonah was the guilty party. He thereon counselled them to cast him into the sea. He was the cause and the cursed; a curse that would only be lifted by lifting him up and throwing him as a victim to the roaring sea. No sooner had the seamen complied with Jonah's request than "the sea ceased from her raging" (Jonah 1:15). Jonah was the last suspected, but once the cause had been detected and expelled, their trouble was behind them.

A missionary who had served the LORD over a period of many years in China near the Tibetan border once told a story well illustrating the principle of diligence in ferreting out sin, and thereby securing answers to prayer and precipitating revival. The missionary had been asked to visit a Buddhist, who was suffering from a chronic sickness or affliction. In the room where the man was bedridden was an effigy of Buddha. Upon seeing it the missionary explained that he would have to get rid of the idol before God would heal him. Reluctantly the sick man agreed to part with it, and prayer for his deliverance was offered, after which the missionary left the house. His return the next day or a little while after found the man still in bed, to the missionary's disappointment. After denying that there were any more idols in the house, the sick man finally admitted that there was an idol in the drawer in that very room. The persistent missionary again stressed that until that idol was destroyed, deliverance was out of the question. Again the Buddhist devotee parted with idol number two and was duly prayed for. The following day the missionary returned, fully expecting to see the patient up and about. He was again nonplussed, whereupon Brother Berulsdan, for such was his name, after plying the Buddhist with further questions, found the man adamant that he had destroyed the last idol, though he was convinced that he had not. After considerable baulking the man eventually admitted there was still one left, and simultaneously reached inside the neck of his robe and pulled out a miniature Buddha suspended from a chain or cord, and handed it to the missionary. Prayer was then offered for the man's deliverance for the third time, and immediately it was answered to the man's satisfaction and the man of God's vindication. It took a threefold delving into the inner life or holds of the ship before the man made a clean breast of his full devotion to the idols which were blocking the way into the presence of God and hindering the return of the angel with the requisite answer to prayer.

Hidden and unconfessed sin is the greatest barrier to answered prayer. So conscious of this is a true Christian in his walk with God that he will go to every length to maintain a conscience void of offence towards God and man. David, in a remarkable phrase ,expressed the sentiment, saying, "I restored that which I took not away" (Psalm 69:4). Rather than leave his accusers convinced of his guilt but unrelenting in their harassment, he acted as if he was guilty and made retribution accordingly. Ours is to make sure that we are carrying no excess baggage or superfluous hindrances. One can be more than tolerably certain that had Rachel divulged that she was the guilty party who had pilfered her father's idols, she would have lived to enjoy Benjamin. Again we opine the words of Jonah coined in the whale's belly: "Those who observe lying vanities forsake their own mercy" (Jonah 2:8).

To have to part with the cargo of grain or wheat must have been a heartbreak to the captain-cum-owner of the ship, but it would have contributed largely to the ship's burden, and as he himself was culpable, having persuaded the centurion to agree to his hauling in the anchors and heading for more spacious winter quarters, his loss was the more galling. He had played for high stakes and lost everything, and but for the goodness of God and the faithfulness of the apostle whose counsel he had scouted, he would have lost his life and his soul into the bargain. His rashness was that of daring to pit his tiny brain against the Word and Providence of God, and therein follow the bent of this world. Paul limns the fashion in familiar words: "Wherein in time past ye walked according to the course of this world, according to the prince of the power of the air" (Ephes.2:2).

For the Christian the disposing of the wheat enforces a moral. One is reminded at the beginning of the story of the doomed ship, that it was registered at Alexandria in Egypt, and was bound for Italy. Not long before the disastrous break-up of the vessel one is reminded that the cargo was one of wheat. Egypt was the main granary of the Roman world, and it is related that during the Neronian persecution of Christians, that so pleasure-mad was the Roman populace that they sent their galleys to Alexandria not for Egypt's golden grain, but for their golden sand to carpet the floor of the amphitheatre to absorb the blood of the Christians slaughtered by the gladiators and wild beasts and by one another. No Roman entertainment was complete without bloodletting, and human at that. Like the people of Sodom their sin was "pride, fullness of bread and abundance of idleness" (Jer.5:8).

Egyptian wheat has its figurative counterpart in the pleasures and entertainments and literature of this world, not excluding the romantic, the pornographic and the copy and matter of the media. On these things the world gluts itself. Its folly is that of seeking happiness in these things and not in God, and in so doing starves the soul. The acme of worldliness is seeking fulfilment and satisfaction in them more than or other than in God. Augustine observed that the soul is dissatisfied until it seeks its satisfaction in Christ alone.

A penetrating question propounded by God in Isaiah is, "Wherefore do ye spend money for that which is not bread and your labour for that which satisfieth not? Hearken ye unto Me and eat that which is good, and let your soul delight itself in fatness" (Isaiah 55:1–2).

From the spiritual and divine standpoint, Egyptian bread is not bread, for the delights and diversions of this life are pseudo forms of happiness, which deceive their patrons. John Keats, one of the nation's greatest poets, and in a poem on the elusive nature of pleasure, wrote:

> Ever let the fancy roam,
> Pleasure never is at home;
> At a touch sweet pleasure melteth,
> Like to bubbles when rain pelteth

They promise much but fail to live up to their extravagant claims. And worse than that, they rob the heart of all desire for God. Christ, using another figure, declared, "No man straightway desireth new wine; for he says the old is better" (Luke 5:39). They are irreconcilable with holiness and purity. So blatant is this the case that the Scripture affirms, "If any man loves the world, the love of the Father is not in him" (1 John 2:10). As is further stated, "He who would be the friend of the world is the enemy of God" (James 4:4). For this there is only one panacea, and that is a clean break with everything that smacks of this world. Cast behind your back everything that would impede your coming to Christ. In the words of the text, "Cast out the wheat into the sea".

In the revival that broke out at Ephesus, "Many of them which used curious arts – or Egyptian wheat – such as members of the occult, brought their books together and burned them before all men: and they counted the price of them, and found it fifty thousand pieces of silver. So mightily grew the Word of the Lord and prevailed" (Acts 19:19– 20). God's wheat or word of the Scriptures is likened to silver. Psalm 12, in its delineation of the Word of God or Scriptures says, "They are pure words as silver tried in a furnace of earth, purified seven times" (verse 6). In his Gospel record Luke intermittently draws attention to the magnetic attraction of the Word of God, of which are subjoined, "And when the people were gathered thick together, he began to say" (Luke 11:29). And again, "In the meantime when there were gathered unto Him an innumerable multitude of people, insomuch that they trode one upon another" (Luke 12:1). To another great company who followed Him, "He turned and said unto them, whoso be he of you that forsaketh not all that he hath, he cannot be My disciple" (Luke 14:26).

God's question in *Isaiah* 55:1–2: "Wherefore do ye spend money for that which is not bread?" begs an answer. As intimated by Christ, who asked Philip, in order to try his faith: "From whence shall we buy bread that all may eat?" (John 6:5–6). As well as having to pay for the grain of the Egypt of this life, it is dearly paid for at that. In the *Revelation* the market price was "one measure of wheat for a penny", which was equivalent to a farm labourer's daily rate (Rev.6:5, 6), in a season of black famine (Matt.20:2). Not only is Egyptian wheat noted for its high prices but, as is true of everything that comes out of the land of Ham, men will spend their strength, ability and wherewithal for that which leaves them dissatisfied.

Another of God's grievances against His people is that they patronise the Egyptians at all, and He expresses His resentment in strong words, saying, "Woe to them that go down to Egypt for help", and in a revealing statement declared, "Now the Egyptians are men and not gods; and their horses flesh and not spirit" (Isaiah 31:3).

Solomon's considerable trade with Egypt was at variance with a clear command to all the kings of Israel. Among them they were forbidden to multiply horses, yet Solomon clearly flouted this for he had chariot cities with fourteen hundred chariots and twelve thousand horsemen, and the price paid was six hundred shekels of silver for a chariot and one hundred and fifty shekels of silver per horse. Solomon's trust was evidently more in chariots and horses than in God. Paul stated the issue with his usual clarity and perspicuity when he wrote to the believers to put on Christ: "But put ye on the LORD Jesus Christ and make no provision for the flesh to fulfil the lusts thereof" (Rom.13:14).

Then mark the stark difference between Egyptian grain and heaven's. The former is costly and has to be bought; heaven's is without money and without price. There is no famine in heaven and God's children can boast, "How many hired servants have my Father with bread to eat and to spare?" (Luke 15:17). Heaven's bread guarantees health and is life-giving. Christ cried, "I am the Living Bread which came down from heaven; if any man shall eat of this bread he shall live for ever" (John 6:5). "He that cometh to Me shall never hunger (John 6:35) and as John Wesley put it, 'that is such and one will be happy and satisfied for ever'". No wonder that Christ advised among other things, "to labour not for the meat or food that perishes" (John 6:27).

Christ's grain is purifying and wholesome. Moses spoke of the grain of Canaan as of such a wholesome nature and this is inferred in an expression which talks of "the fat of the kidneys of wheat" (Deut.32:14). The function of the kidneys is to purify the bloodstream, which carries life to every organ in the body and thereby purifies and vitalises them. By the bread of heaven – the heavenly Canaan – the very life of Christ is assimilated and inwardly renews the believer (2 Cor.4:16).

A clear duty for all those who would secure salvation is to dump the wheat of this world into the sea of God's judgement, as that which is anathema to Him. For "the ingredients of its bread or wheat are, 'the lusts of the flesh' – appetite – 'the lusts of the eyes' – avarice – and 'the pride of life' – ambition" (C. H. Mellors). God's judgements are likened to "a great deep" (Psalm 36:6) which is supplemented by Paul's expression of wonder: "O the depth of the riches both of the wisdom and knowledge of God. How unsearchable are His judgements and His ways past finding out!" (Rom.11:33). It was poetic justice that Egyptian wheat be dumped in the sea, for fifteen hundred years earlier, the long-suffering justice of God had disposed of the martial might of Egypt in the Red Sea. The citation reads, "Pharaoh's chariots and his hosts hath He cast into the sea; his chosen captains also hath He drowned in the Red Sea. The depths have covered them; they sank into the bottom as a stone" (Exodus 15:4–5).

To cast away, therefore, all the items that nourished the old life of Adam, who corrupted himself and his descendants by eating from a forbidden tree, which was a mixture of knowledge both good and evil, is imperative for the gaining of salvation through faith in Christ alone, "For if any man is in Christ, he is a new creature, old things are passed away, behold all things are become new" (2 Cor.5:17).

* * * * * * ** * * * * * * * * * *

SERMON 22

LAND AHOY

Acts 27:39: *And when it was day, they knew not the land: but they discovered a certain creek with a shore, into which they were minded, if it were possible to thrust in the ship.*

Paul's prognostication was fully vindicated. By the light of day the crew could descry the island that would provide them with a safe and suitable haven, though ignorant of its name. In a figure it was a revelation of the Gospel Day and is in contrast to this life, or the life of nature without Christ; alternatively, the darkness of the human heart when devoid of the life of Christ. It explains, therefore, that while people have an awareness of the religion of Christ, yet they are perfectly ignorant of the salvation enshrined in the Gospel with all its beatific blessings. Several instances of this paradox crop up in the Bible. Although Christ is disclosed, yet many are woefully ignorant.

A glaring example of ignorance though surrounded by the dazzling light of truth is that of the stupidity of Peter and John on the morning of Christ's resurrection. Mary Magdalene had brought the dramatic if not traumatic news of the missing body of Christ from the tomb, saying, "They have taken away the Lord out of the sepulchre, and we know not where they have laid Him" (John 20:2). Such startling news sent the two foremost disciples running to the sepulchre, and they found the tomb open with the linen clothes exactly as described by Mary Magdalene, and this was further substantiated by a closer examination. Wonderingly they departed, after which, it is said, "they saw and believed". What they believed is supported by the qualifying Scripture, viz., they believed what the women had told them – that some unknown persons had exhumed the body – which construction is insisted upon by the explanatory statement, "For as yet, they knew not the Scripture, that He must rise again from the dead" (John 20:8–9). Christ had said on several occasions that although He would be delivered into the hands of wicked men and crucified and slain, He would rise again from the dead, which so exasperated Peter that he expostulated roundly, "Be it far from Thee LORD" (Matt.16:21–3), so that while they knew of the Scripture, they had never grasped its significance or experienced its power. To them it was not a reality.

It was only when Peter came to himself that he realised it was no vision or dream, that he had been let out of prison by the angel, to a place with which he was familiar. "Upon reflection, he took his bearings and proceeded to the house of Mary and John Mark" (Acts 12:9–12).

In spite of his residence in the Temple and surrounded by those things which were latent with Gospel truth, such as the Ark of the Covenant, which with other articles was the repository of the tablets inscribed with the Ten Commandments by the finger of God, and given to Moses on Mount Sinai, it is surprisingly written, "Now Samuel did not yet know the LORD, neither was the Word of the LORD revealed to him" (1 Sam.3:7). His reaction to the call of God as he lay on his pallet bears out this anomaly. Four times God called to him before he answered and then, only after Eli the paramount priest had primed him to respond in a phrase with which every Sunday school scholar is able to quote, namely, "Speak LORD for Thy servant heareth". Even then the lad was remiss, for his reply was "Speak for Thy servant heareth". One word had been left out, which was the vital word "LORD" (1 Sam.3:10). Nor is this strange: if as the Scripture says "No man can call Jesus LORD but by the holy Ghost" (1 Cor.12:3), his having not the Spirit disqualified him from addressing the LORD in that familiar manner.

Though the dawn of a new Gospel Day has broken upon the world, millions who see the land are utterly devoid of its real meaning and spiritual purport envisaged in Christ (verse 39). On the day that Christ rode into Jerusalem on a donkey, as long foretold by Zechariah the prophet (Zech.9:9), it is reported that all the city was moved, Zechariah saying, "Who is this?" Although He was their king, fondly hoped for and expected, they knew Him not. From the days of Jacob they had been apprised of His advent, who while giving the patriarchal blessing to his sons on his dying bed ejaculated, "I have waited for Thy salvation O LORD" (Gen.49:18). Ironically that salvation was the cardinal reason for His advent. Zechariah declared that "their King is meek and having salvation".

When Paul came to Ephesus, he found in the city about a dozen persons who said they were disciples of the LORD, who when questioned by the apostle confessed they had never heard of the Holy Ghost (Acts 19:2–5).

One redeeming feature of the discerned land was the sight of a creek with a shore which offered the crew more than a plausible hope of entering and wedging the ship if not firmly mooring it, without which their danger would have been as great as ever and this would certainly have been the case if it had been a sheer rock-faced cliff down to the water's edge. The proverb: "Out of the frying pan and into the fire" would have been their lot. A story is told of a ship being driven by gale-force winds towards the rock face of the Isle of Bressay off the Shetland Isles. Frantically the crew climbed onto the rigging, and from that vantage point noticed a rope ladder hanging from the top of the cliff. Men had been working in the slate quarry below and had abandoned their site because of the storm which had made their position hazard-ous. In their haste they forgot to remove the ladder, which was, without doubt, providentially provided for the storm-tossed ship. Presently the storm drove them near to the rope ladder on the rock face. One by one they leaped from the rigging to the rope ladder and clambered to the cliff top. There was not a single casualty, but by morning the vessel had been smashed and completely broken up through the battering it had received from the merciless sea.

As the crew looked anxiously in the morning light and saw the above-mentioned creek, with the shore, their relief must have been great. Like the foregoing story it could only have been a divinely arranged escape hatch. Once out of the ship and the sea they would be safe on the shore. God's deliverances are never rough and ready but most invariably smooth and available. Jeremiah was, in the nick of time, hauled out of the miry dungeon with cords and cast-clouts. God's mercies are always tender mercies and His kindnesses are loving-kindnesses (Psalm 103:4).

Great skill and concentration, to say nothing of courage, would still be demanded to negotiate a successful landing. So tricky was the operation involved that from a natural standpoint it could easily miscarry. It is worded, "If it were possible". In any undertaking involving danger there is never lacking an element of uncertainty, or of last-minute hitches, especially when such an undertaking has never been attempted before. In the current saga, needless to say, there is another dimension, and that other dimension is divine, of whom Christ said, "All things are possible, only believe", which eliminates all possibility of failure. Paul had put it down in black and white: "I can do all things through Christ which strengtheneth me" (Phil.4:13). God's ability and involvement is such that He can bring us ashore without making the sea calm, even while it still rages and the winds are howling a requiem and there are no life jackets.

Thrusting is expressive of force used to overcome resistance or opposition or opposing forces. With the sea still in an angry mood, laced with counter currents and possibly crosswinds, it was essential for the men to develop sufficient momentum to achieve their purpose. To enter the kingdom of heaven demands determination. Christ reminded His hearers of such fixity of heart, saying, "From the days of John the Baptist until now" – that is until the kingdom of Christ – "the kingdom of God suffereth violence and the violent take it by force", which force has been likened to an army storming a city after the walls have been breached, for which action the Roman legions were masters. Military history leaves on record the superb gallantry of one of its famous legionaries who had been the first to mount the breach forty times, and had been decorated more than 200 times, but the price paid for his daring was that of numerous wounds. Of the woman who had suffered for twelve years with chronic bleeding, it is written that her haemorrhaging stopped immediately after she had pressed through the throng, aptly called 'the press', and touched Christ's robe. The pressure she exerted must needs pit itself against the pressure of the crowd, who were as determined to stop her getting through as she was to obtain healing by tapping the source of His virtue. Weak as she was after twelve years of losing blood, her strength of purpose won through. Always the greatest hindrance to godliness is the crowd or the press. Prayer and faith alone overcome opposition, whether it be demonic, critical or family. Among Christ's most relentless critics were His own family. On one occasion His mother and other members of His family disturbed Him as he was teaching in a home in Capernaum demanding that he come outside. A half-hearted approach to the Gospel, and the salvation enshrined within it will splutter out like a damp squib.

To thrust in the ship, therefore, was a derring-do exercise. Failure at the first attempt would be disastrous; there would be no room for further manoeuvre. If the crew missed the inlet they would be hurled onto the rocks that skirted the shore, not unlike the spacecraft returning to the earth. Its entry into the earth's atmosphere was gauged to a specific angle. Should they miscalculate and enter the atmosphere zone at a wrong angle they would be hurled off at a tangent and go spinning into space on an endless journey from which return was impossible.

One of the pathetic failures in this respect was the wealthy and personable young nobleman who came earnestly to Christ with, as it were, all masts fully rigged. It is said "He came running", fully determined to thrust in his vessel into the creek. Sadly, he missed the opening – a creek – a narrow inlet: Christ called it the eye of a needle. Ominously, the nobleman had not lightened the ship of its cargo of gold. It became unmanageable and failed to respond to the wheel or tiller, and was deflected. Christ's rueful comment to His disciples was, "How hardly shall they that have riches enter the kingdom of God." Such, however, is not impossible, "For with God all things are possible" (Matt.19:26).

* * * * * * * * * * * * * * * * * * * *

SERMON 23

ACTION STATIONS

Acts 27:40: *They made towards shore.*

The crew's situation was like the lawyer who answered Christ wisely and received an encouraging answer, and was told, "I perceive that thou art not far from the kingdom". Neither was their situation dissimilar from that of the disciples, when approaching land after a night's fishing failure. Land was a mere 200 cubits away, but they failed to recognise the LORD, who stood, solitarily, on the otherwise abandoned beach.

Salvation was within their grasp, as God's salvation is never remote in either time or place. "Behold now is the accepted time; behold now is the day of salvation" (2 Cor.6:2), "For the grace of God that bringeth salvation hath appeared to all men" (Titus 2:11–12).

Their first exercise was to lift the anchors: they had become redundant. "Hope that is seen is not hope, but if we hope for that which we see not, then do we with patience wait for it" (Rom.8:24–5). A like sentiment is expressed by Jeremiah, whose patience had been stretched to the limit: "It is good that a man should both hope and quietly wait for the salvation of the LORD" (Lam.3:26). The day the storm-tossed mariners and passengers had waited for, when they would exchange the creaking and greasy boards beneath their feet for terra firma, had dawned. Hope had taken visible shape. The anchors were no longer needed. Spread out in front of them was the shore of salvation. Verily, "the darkness was past and the true light was now shining" (1 John 2:8).

The second step was to commit themselves to the sea; not

to chance or to Lady Luck, but to that element called sea or ocean that is directed and controlled by the providence of God. Job complained to God querulously, "Am I a sea or a whale that Thou settest a watch against me?" (Job 7:2). Actually men need to be watched with their deceitful hearts, far more than old ocean. Men are the least beings to be trusted among the creatures of this world. Heavenly watchers have their eyes focussed day and night, like the cameras dispersed along the motorways (Dan.4:17). God has His own invisible barriers to contain and restrict the sea, as implied in the question that He put to the perturbed patriarch: "Who shut up the sea with doors, when it brake forth, as if it had issued out of the womb? When I made the cloud the garment thereof, and thick darkness a swaddling-band for it, And brake up for it my decreed place, and set bars and doors, And said, 'Hitherto shalt thou come, but no further: and here shall thy proud waves be stayed?'" (Job 38:8–11). God, strikingly, likens the emergence of the sea as of a baby emerging from the womb, and immediately confined to a cot, otherwise the sea's basin, with its protective sides, after its having been swaddled with clouds as a garment. So controlled is it by God's providence that it cannot go beyond God's appointed border, as decreed by His order. "God's steps are said to be in the great waters and His footsteps – or prints – are not known" (Psalm 77:19), for He never leaves any. Among the wonders that men see when they go down to the sea in ships is that of the tempest that He stirs up and later subdues, "He commandeth and raiseth up the stormy wind, which lifteth up the waves thereof … He maketh the storm a calm, so that the waves thereof be still; So He bringeth them unto their desired haven" (Psalm 107:25–30).

When they committed themselves to the sea they were in effect committing themselves to the providence of God, and in so doing to His salvation. In the same manner the king of Nineveh and his subjects cast themselves on the mercy of God, in spite of the want of encouragement, "And God repented of the evil He would do, and He did it not" (Jonah 3:10).

Imperative to the success of their venture was the operation of loosing the rudder bands, which has been explained as the helm or steering gear of the ship, which were two paddles on each side of the stern of the ship. When not in use they were hauled out of the water and secured to its sides. James likens the tongue to the helm of a ship, which although very small, turns it about even when driven by fierce winds. "Even so," says James, "the tongue is a little member and boasteth great things," which without the help of God is untameable, and which has two options, "therewith bless we God, even the Father; and therewith curse we men" (James 3:4–10). Apart, however, from the ungovernable nature of the tongue, in normal situations there are certain factors that can and do influence and even control it, in addition to God's intervention. Attention is drawn to rudder bands which bind the paddles or helm when not in use. These have their counterparts in the controlling of behaviour of the tongue. Two elements that affect its usage are the fear of man or the influence of the favour of man. To explain more fully, as pointed out in the proverb: "The fear of man bringeth a snare" (Prov.29:35), while the favour of man, as in the proffering of a bribe or a position of honour, "perverteth justice" (1 Sam.8:3).

In the matter of man's salvation, the tongue plays a leading part. Just as the rudder of a ship controls its direction, so the tongue is the determining factor whether the individual goes to heaven or hell. Precisely for this reason the Christian calling is denominated "the profession or confession of faith" (1 Tim.6:12–13). Paul's two steps in salvation, set forth in the letter to the *Romans*, are verbal testimony and belief or trust. A much quoted scripture reads, "If thou shalt confess with thy mouth the LORD Jesus, and shalt believe in thine heart that God hath raised Him from the dead, thou shalt be saved. For with the heart man believeth unto righteousness; and with the mouth confession is made unto salvation ... For there is no difference between the Jew and the Greek: for the same LORD over all is rich unto all that call upon Him. For whosoever shall call upon the LORD shall be saved" (Rom.10:9–13). "But what saith it? The Word is nigh thee, even in thy mouth, and in thy heart: that is, the word of faith, which we preach" (Rom.10:8).

Often has the fear of men inhibited many from confessing Christ publicly, or kept them back from a public profession, by identifying Christ in water baptism, which is a bold and open method of nailing their colours to the mast, and asserting that they have become followers of Christ. Their message is that they have changed their allegiance from self-serving to God pleasing, and are steering for heaven. In his Gospel John observed that among the chief rulers also many believed; but because of the Pharisees they did not confess Him lest they should be put out of the synagogue "... for they loved the praise of men more than the praise of God" (John 12:42–3). Their tongues were silenced – bound – because the price of losing popularity and the moral credit of their spiritual mentors was too high. It took Nicodemus virtually the whole period of Christ's three years of public ministry before he emerged from the ivory palace of popular esteem to take sides with the scorned and despised Christ of Galilee, and with Joseph of Arithmathæa openly confess Him without fear. He who first came clandestinely, if not furtively, to seek an audience with Jesus by night was too ashamed and tongue-tied to seek Him out in broad daylight (John 3:1–2). Until the rudder bands are loosed there can be no progress to the creek of salvation, or eventually to heaven, and without the rudder the vessel would be going around in circles.

Simultaneously they hoisted the mainsail to the wind. Christ said, "The wind bloweth where it listeth", and by the wind He meant the Holy Ghost or the Spirit of God. Wind is produced by a current of air flowing from a high pressure build-up to a lower one. The greater the differential of air build-up then the more powerful is the flow. A gale is caused by great extremes of pressure. A major phenomenon of the Day of Pentecost was that of the sound of a rushing mighty wind which filled all the house where a 120 disciples were sitting. Heaven is the high pressure centre of the breath of the Spirit of God, and contrasts strongly with the hearts of men, yet hungry and thirsty for God, and explains the rushing sound. Between two extremes on that day the vacuum in the hearts of the disciples was responsible for the powerful flow from the throne of God or the Seven Spirits which were before the throne, representing "the seven-fold graces of the one eternal and Holy Spirit" (Isaiah 11:2– 3). Christ said, "The wind bloweth where it listeth". Its bent or direction is the human heart when the heart is conditioned for its reception. Consequently it is the chief agent in bringing sinners to Christ, who said, "He shall glorify Me" and in the same breath, "He shall guide you into all truth … He shall take of the things of Mine and reveal them unto you" (John 16:13, 15). Paul wrote, "Know ye not that the unrighteous shall not inherit the kingdom of God?" After listing ten vices of the unrighteous he unsparingly indicted the Corinthians with an abrasive censure: "And such were some of you", but immediately tempers his accusation with the mollifying words of comfort: "But ye are washed, but ye are sanctified, but ye are justified, in the name of the LORD Jesus, and by the Spirit of our God" (1 Cor.6:9–11).

A conditioned heart implies a heart whose desire is for God and thus heavenly in its direction. In the closing scenes of this shipwreck story the heavenly bias is equated in the phrase "and hoisted up the mainsail to the wind" (verse 40), which is figurative of the exhortation "Set your affections or seek those things which are above, not on things on the earth, where Christ sitteth on the right hand of God" (Col.3:1–2). By the mainsail is meant a loving heart. Of all the virtues love is the main one, and is defined so by the apostle in his encomium of charity, in which he concludes, "And now abideth faith, hope, charity, these three; but the greatest of these is charity" (1 Cor.13:13). And as the mariners hoisted the mainsail and unfurled it, so those who desire heaven's salvation must set their sails to catch the heavenly breeze. Of all the duties and charges that make up the Sermon on the Mount, that which is given the pre-eminence and which comprises all the others is: "But seek ye first the kingdom of God, and His righteousness; and all these things shall be added unto you" (Matt.6:33). In that same homily Christ had reminded them that heavenly treasure alone enjoyed immunity from depredators or depreciation through erosion, and that "where one's treasure was there would be their hearts also" (Matt.6:21).

The hoisting of the sail symbolised their affection towards the shore, which was their hearts' longings would be realised and their hearts' ease. For fourteen days and nights they had experienced considerable uneasiness, which had eclipsed their physical discomfort and was agitated by the constancy of the storm and the battering of the giant rollers, so that the now clearly discerned shore promised peace and security, associated with an island or place of refuge, in spite of cold and drenching rain. In the fourth chapter of the epistle to the *Hebrews* the writer made repeated references to "the rest that remains to the people of God" and drew attention to the people of God in the wilderness forfeiting it because of their unbelief, and couched in monotonously recurring words: "So, we see they could not enter in because of their unbelief" (Heb.3:19). In a final word on the subject Paul stressed its importance by a further exhortation, saying, "Let us labour, therefore, to enter into that rest, lest any man fall after the same example of unbelief" (Heb.4:11), or though differently worded, but offering the same salvation, "that we might have strong consolation, who have fled for refuge to lay hold of the hope set before us" (Heb.6:18). An eminent writer has noted "that the language depicts the distress of a battered ship, the object of many storms, and entering the veil, to lay hold of Christ the subject of our hope and the glory we hope for through Him" (Heb.6:18).

* * * * * * * * * * * * * * * * * * *

SERMON 24

A PLACE WHERE TWO SEAS MET

Acts 27:41: *And falling into a place where two seas met, they ran the ship aground, and the forepart stuck fast, and remained immoveable, but the hinder part was broken with the violence of the waves.*

God in His providence had contrived a creek by the interaction of two tides or currents which had eroded the rock face at their point of contact. In turn the particles of rock or sand thus ground had accumulated to form a shore or beach, leaving a fissure in the rock. Moses was placed in such a fissure or cleft formed by God, in a rock where he had been charged to stand. Concerning that vantage point God had said, "There is a place by Me, in that place I will cause My glory to pass before thee, and I will proclaim the name of the LORD before thee". God called it cleft by Him and it had its derivation in a root word which means a place of refuge. In the Canticle of Solomon, the Beloved called the Shulamite "His dove" and remarked that she was "in the cleft of the rock and in the secret places of the stairs" (Song of Sol.2:14), which Watchman Nee in his book on the Song of Solomon alludes to as the spouse's (meaning the believer's) identity with her Beloved (meaning Christ) in His death and resurrection as spoken of in Ephes. 2:5, 6.

Repeatedly Christ is revealed as the Rock, or sometimes the Stone. Peter refers to Him as the latter, in his saying "to whom coming as unto a Living Stone", and, in a further paragraph, writing "Behold I lay in Zion a chief corner stone, elect and precious: and He that believeth on Him shall not be confounded" or stumble (1 Pet.2:4–6). Paul's contribution runs: "And they drank of that spiritual rock that followed them, and that Rock was Christ" (1 Cor.10:4).

Moses in his song uses the name Jeshurun for the people of Israel. This is the term of endearment, but the song then goes on to say, "That he waxed fat and kicked and forsook God the Rock of his salvation" (Deut.32:15). Typically, then, the creek that had been carved out by the coalescence of two powerful currents may be viewed as the refuge provided for storm-tossed moral delinquents and the terminology used to describe the whereabouts of that refuge is identical to that used by the composer of Psalm 85, in which Psalm he points out that "Mercy and truth are met together; righteousness and peace have kissed each other" (Psalm 85:10). Those attributes are at the extremities of the spectrum of the light and character of God, and would seem to be irreconcilable. God's righteousness or truth are relentlessly and vociferously demanding justice against the offenders of God's holy law, while mercy and peace are earnest suppliants entreating for clemency, and endlessly so. Both may be likened to the measureless oceans of God's holiness and character. God's judgements or righteous principles are called a great deep (Psalm 36:6). God's love is construed as a measureless ocean by Paul, who prayed for the Christians of Ephesus that "they might comprehend with all saints what is the breadth and length and depth and height of the love of God which passeth knowledge" (Ephes.3:18–19). A parallel is clearly discernable between the place where two seas met and formed a creek or a narrow inlet which provided a safe haven to the distressed grain ship with the tide of God's justice and the tide of His mercy, which did not collide but colluded in Christ at Golgotha and together carved out an asylum of refuge. Well may it be said of the crisis of the Christ suspended by nails from the cross at the place of the skull, "Mercy and truth are met together, righteousness and peace have kissed each other". In Christ they are united in an eternal embrace; joined together by the kiss of eternal reconciliation. The marriage was solemnized at the altar of God, or the cross of Christ, when the Roman sword rived the side of Christ's body and released the supernatural build-up of blood and water. Together the blood and the water made provision through Christ from the power of sin and death and hell. What started out as a wanton and sacrilegious action of the Roman legionary in gouging a rent in the body of Christ that was a hand's breadth in length became the consolidating of the union which would have allowed Thomas to have thrust in his hand had he taken Christ at His word.

David's refuge for his 600 distressed and harassed malcontents was the cave Adullam, meaning 'the justice of the people' and echoes the salvation of that heavenly Adullam Rock Christ Jesus, and explained by Paul with his gifted insight: "But now the righteousness of God without the Law is manifested, being witnessed by the Law and the Prophets; even the righteousness of God which is by the faith of Jesus Christ unto all and upon all that believe ... being justified freely by His grace through the redemption which is in Christ Jesus, whom God hath set forth to be a propitiation, through faith in His blood ... to declare, I say, at this time, His righteousness: that He might be just and the justifier of him which believeth in Jesus" (Rom.3:21–6).

God said to Noah, "And the door of the Ark thou shalt set in the side thereof" (Gen 6:18). It was built to provide a secure storm-proof refuge from the impending storm of divine wrath, into which access was provided by a solitary door let into the side. Salvation from the wrath that is to come is for all who fall into the place where the two seas meet, that is the side of Christ from which when pierced blood and water flowed out: "It is the blood that makes atonement for the soul and the water of Christ's Word that sanctifies wholly" (F. B. Meyer).

They were said, "to have fallen into a place where two seas met". Falling is defined as free descent, which attitude is implied in the humility required to identify with Christ. For this reason the apostle exhorted the Philippians to "Let the mind of Christ dwell in them, who became obedient to death, even the death of the cross". Christ offered no resistance which the action of falling requires (Phil.2:5, 8).

Then they deliberately ran the ship aground to provide them with a stable and solid state unrocked by the boisterous elements. A first requirement of a Christian is stability, of which Christ is the supreme example, depicted as "Jesus Christ the same yesterday, today and for ever" (Heb.13:8). Paul, after reciting his many harsh afflictions, played them down in a revealing aphorism, saying, "But none of these things move me" (Acts 20:24). To his Ephesian converts he wrote, "That ye be henceforth no more children tossed to and fro, and carried about with every wind of doctrine, by the sleight of men, and cunning craftiness whereby they lie in wait to deceive" (Ephes.4:14). But because of the victory believers in Christ have over sin and death, they are charged to be steadfast and unmoveable, always abounding in the work of the LORD" (1 Cor.15:58). In grounding the vessel the desired end was gained: "The forepart stuck fast" (verse 41).

In the typology of the story the forepart relates to the future experience and destiny of all those who have cast themselves upon the LORD. "A Christian's future is secure as long as they hold fast the beginning of their confidence steadfast unto the head" (Heb.3:6, 14). The Gospel message is focussed around a future life, and the reality of an eternal existence. Among the several denominated fools of the Bible is the rich man who had a problem with his wealth, and soliloquised, "What shall I do with my goods?" Finally he opted for an enlargement of the infrastructure of his estate and an early retirement. His possessions were more than adequate to maintain his present state and luxurious standard of living for many years. Therein lay his presumption and folly. That same night he died, having made no preparation for his soul, or taken serious thought for eternity, which, incidentally, is not restricted solely to the wealthy, but is often the folly of the generality of mankind.

Although Job was a chronically sick man yet he echoed far loftier sentiments than the wealthy magnate of the parable – sentiments which have been immortalised in a book more durable than anything chiselled in marble, saying, "For I know that my redeemer liveth . . and though after my skin worms destroy this body, yet in my flesh shall I see God, whom I shall see for myself, and mine eyes shall behold and not another" (Job 19:23–7). After all, the first business of life is preparing for the inevitable, the ultimate and the eternal.

Just as positively as the bows of the ship held as firmly as if in a vice, so surely did the hinder part break up quickly "by the violence of the waves"; it may be truly said that the hinder part of a Christian's lot covers that period from his accountability as a moral agent to God to the moment of surrendering his life to Christ. Every person's life is summed up in the thumbnail sketch of Paul's opening verses of *Ephesians* Chapter Two, the tenor of which, the common denominator of all and sundry, without exception is, "And you hath He quickened who were dead in trespasses and sins, wherein in time past ye walked according to the course of this world, according to the prince of the power of the air, the spirit that now worketh in the children of disobedience" (Ephes.2:1–2). And as the hinder part or stern of the ship was soon submerged under the water, having succumbed to the violence of the waves, so when a person comes in repentance to God and faith in Christ, all the past life is delivered the *coup-de-grace* and ceases to be, "For if any man be in Christ, old things", be they ideas, principles, convictions, aspirations, practices, pleasures, "are passed away like the melting snow in spring-sunshine" (John Wesley). "Behold all things are become new" (2 Cor.5:17).

Both Orpah and Ruth accompanied Naomi on her return to Bethlehem, and both were of the same mind to quit their homeland of Moab. By the time, however, that they reached the border, Orpah had a change of mind, which surfaced when Naomi tested the depth of their committal by emphasising the greatness of the sacrifice they would be making if they proceeded any further. With seeming reluctance Orpah wilted and took a tearful farewell of her mother-in-law. She loved Naomi but not her God. Contrariwise Ruth stuck to her like a limpet, and no entreaties or arguments could budge her from her entrenched position. She had nailed her colours to the mast, having fallen in love with Naomi and her God. Her famous and heart-moving asseveration of loyalty was listed in nine affirmations of attachment to Naomi personally, of which the kingpin was, "Thy God shall be my God" (Ruth 1:16–17). Orpah returned to her past and disappeared in oblivion; Ruth went on to a glorious future and ongoing continuity, with her name enrolled in the Bible and in the heavenly register.

God's waves of judgement will dispense relentless justice upon the stubbornly impenitent, whose attachment to the old life stifled all their erstwhile desires for a brand new life in Christ, even in this present evil world, and an ongoing one in the City of God with its imperishable foundations and invaluable infrastructure, concerning which God had said: "Behold I make all things new" (Rev.21:5–6), and added a qualifying rider, "He that overcometh shall inherit all things" – literally 'all these new things'.

* *

SERMON 25

SATAN'S PLOT FOILED

Acts 27:42–3: *And the soldiers' counsel was to kill the prisoners, lest any of them should swim out, and escape. But the centurion, willing to save Paul, kept them from their purpose; and commanded that they which could swim should cast themselves first into the sea, and get to land.*

Satan had contrived Paul's death at Jerusalem: first by lynching at the hands of a Jewish mob, which Claudius Lysias had barely prevented with a small army, and literally snatching Paul from their hands. Shortly after, a band of more than forty fanatical Jews intrigued with the Jewish leaders to bring the prisoner to Jerusalem under the guise of a further questioning, but would lie in wait to set upon him and kill him. Together they had placed themselves under a great curse that they would not eat until the assassination of the apostle was accomplished. Paul's nephew got wind of it and reported the plot first to the apostle and then to Lysias. Immediately Paul was smuggled to Cæsarea. Satan next endeavoured to sink the boat by stirring up a prolonged tempest, causing the loss of all on board without trace. Enraged by the prospect of their being soon home and dry, that wicked one stirred up the soldiers to demand the forfeiture of the lives of all the prisoners, to ensure there would be no escapees, for which Roman discipline would have held them accountable. And it is surmised that the centurion would have had no scruples in carrying out their wishes. As their commanding officer, he would probably have been court-martialed. So enamoured was he, however, of Paul, that he asserted his authority, to prevent Paul sharing their fate. Nor is the brutality and ungratefulness of the soldiers to be marvelled at. If the basic instinct of every creature, both animal and human, is self-preservation, then men brutalized by war and carnage can hardly be expected to shed any tears over the mass killings of those who could occasion their own deaths. Even so, to say the least, the soldiers were culpable of gross ingratitude, firstly towards the LORD and secondly towards Paul, who had been the instrument of their salvation thus far. They provide a vivid example of the selfish stance of mankind generally to the God of heaven and earth "Who spared not His own Son but delivered Him up for us all, and who with Him also freely gives us all things" (Rom.8:32). Yet, far from being placated, they continue in open rebellion (Rom.1:32). Understandable, therefore, is the sentiment of the proverb: "Let favour be shewed to the wicked, yet will he not learn righteousness" (Isaiah 26:10). Among all the demonstrations of ingratitude there are few to equal the dastardly action of Joash, king of Judah, of whom is recorded that "Joash the king remembered not the kindness which Jehoiada his father had done to him, but slew his son Zechariah" (2 Chron.24:22).

How true is the aphorism that "for the sake of one good man – God will preserve the lives of many wicked". Because of Jehoshaphat's high standing with the LORD, the wholesale death by thirst of three armies in the desert that was contiguous with the country of Moab, was staved off by the vocal ministry of Elisha (2 Kings 3:10–18).

Paul's testimony had a long future in front of it, and bore out one of Wesley's many apt sayings: "A man is immortal until his work is done". Until then numerous hazards would punctuate his ongoing service, in spite of which he would keep bouncing back. In any case, the suggestion of the prisoners making a break for freedom was preposterous. On a small island like Malta they would soon have been rounded up.

Once the venomous demands of the soldiers had been curbed, orders were given by Julius to "all who could swim to cast themselves first into the sea and get to land". In the Bible swimming is a figure of the exercise of believing prayer, which bespeaks a heavenly attitude. Ezekiel, in his description of the river that flowed from under the threshold of the house, likened the progressive and uniform stages of the river, each separated by a thousand cubits, to the differing expressions of the Christian calling. Each section contained an equal depth of water, gradually deepening from ankle depth to knees and loins, but after that they became impassable, and described their depth as "risen waters", with an additional clarification, saying, "They were water to swim in" (Ezek.47:1–5), "even a river that could not be passed over". The risen waters of the Spirit of God will launch people heavenwards and powerfully inspire them to pray. Paul was overwhelmed with a deep sense of remorse when Jesus revealed Himself to him on the Damascus high road, and who told him to go to a street called Straight to the home of one named Judas, from where he would receive his marching orders. For the next three days he was immured in that home, in great darkness of body and mind and the latter in a turmoil. To this man in deep distress Ananias was sent by the LORD, to minister to his spiritual need and bring him to a state of salvation – Christ said to Ananias, "Behold he prayeth". His reputation until then was that of a perse-cutor of whom it could be said, "Behold, he persecuteth", as yet he had seen Christ but was not in Him, which was the expression he was so fond of using after he became a Christian (2 Cor.12:2). His bent and desire were heavenward; his feet were off the ground. Risen waters were lifting him up.

When speaking of the judgement of Moab, God revealed to Isaiah that "in the Mount of the LORD [Mount Zion] Moab should be trodden down, and God would spread forth His hands in the midst of them as he that swimmeth spreadeth forth his hands to swim" (Isaiah 25:11).

Solomon's prayer, which he prayed at the dedication of the Temple, is the longest prayer in the Bible. Its theme was that in any foreseeable situation of need or crisis of private persons or the nation as a whole, God would answer prayer and accede to their desires when they made the sacred edifice the focal point of their petitions and looked to heaven His dwelling place, which plea was honoured by God as long as the Temple was standing. Jonah from the whale's belly looked towards God's holy temple, calling upon God to deliver him from his eerie entombment – a request which was immediately granted. Daniel, knowing of the king's decree to punish by consigning to a den of lions all who ignored the king's decree and prayed to any other god but himself for a set month's period, went to his chamber, where his window was always open towards Jerusalem, as had been his habit, and prayed three times daily. God so honoured his prayer that His angel was sent to shut the mouths of the lions. All through the intervening centuries from its dedication to its destruction God kept faith with His promise to Solomon. All the time the king was praying, his posture was a kneeling one with his hands spread out towards heaven. To this bearing, attention is drawn to it, both at the beginning and at the end of his protracted supplication (1 Kings 8:22–54).

Such an action bespeaks that of a swimmer who with his hands sweeps away the hindering element simultaneously as his feet push away the water from him thereby giving propulsion to the body. When men are in earnest about the salvation of their souls their eagerness will be expressed in like language to Paul's: "Brethren this one thing I do, forgetting those things which are behind and reaching forth to those things which are before, I press toward the mark for the prize of the high calling of God in Christ Jesus" (Phil.3:13–14). No one ever gained salvation and finally heaven without believing prayer.

Every baby is born crying, unless stillborn. The first duty of a midwife is to cause the collapsed lungs to expand; producing the cry made possible by its inhaling the vital breath we call oxygen or air.

If every baby is born crying, so every believer is born again praying and crying Abba-Father. When the prodigal in the parable left home for the far country, the word 'father' dropped out of his vocabulary. Only when he came to himself, and a correct reappraisal of his woebegone state came over him, did he resume the thread of the language of home. Not only did he decide to return home immediately but to resume the language of his forfeited relationship. He had voluntarily abandoned his home and family ties. So much was the case that his father bemoaned him as one dead after his willful separation, and upon his return, said, harking back to that sad parting, "This my son was dead". Before he turned for home and took the first step back, he rehearsed to himself what he would say. "I will say Father", which when he could blurt out his confession, after being smothered with his father's compassion and kisses, continued, "I have sinned against heaven and in thy sight. I am no more worthy to be called thy son" (Luke 15:21).

Cornelius of Cæsarea was given to constant prayer. He is said to have "prayed to God always" (Acts 10:2). To this Roman centurion an angel of God was dispatched to tell him that his prayers and his alms had come up for a memorial before God, "And that if he would send to Joppa for one named Simon Peter that he would tell him words whereby he and all his house would be saved" (Acts 10:13–14). Cornelius had so habituated himself to prayer that it led him to salvation. Not one whit less was the earnest appeal of the thief on the cross: "LORD remember me when Thou comest into Thy kingdom". He was the only man of all that cosmopolitan crowd who prayed that day, to whom the LORD gave immediate priority, saying "Verily I say unto thee, today shalt thou be with Me in Paradise" (Luke 27:42–8). Like Christ, his hands were nailed to the cross. He spread or stretched out his hands of prayer and laid hold of salvation and eternal life.

In telling them first to cast themselves into the sea and get to land, the centurion wisely deduced that those who did so would be examples and inspirations to the others who would be more timorous because of their fear of breasting the water. A praying person will always inspire others to emulate him.

Attention is drawn to Rebekah's barrenness, because of which Isaac entreated the LORD for her, and was successful in his appeal, so that she within a little conceived. Complications, notwithstanding, set in, and a perplexed Rebekah asked, "Why am I thus?" That is, she asked Isaac. His inability to give her a satisfactory answer drove her to the LORD, and she was given information regarding twins in her womb who would become two nations of radically opposite temperaments and dispositions, in which the law of *primo geniture* would no longer operate, but from then the elder would be subordinate to the younger. Isaac, for once, was out of touch with God and His future programme, and did his utmost to countermand it, only to be confounded by God.

Shakespeare in *Twelfth Night* said, "some men are born great, some achieve greatness, and some have greatness thrust upon them". Of the latter class is the small body of heroes who have made their mark for God, for it is not given to all men to be leaders or pioneers, but once given a bold and clear lead many will take courage and follow.

Judah had been chosen to lead Israel for forty years through an inhospitable desert little better than a death trap. "In the first place went the standard of the camp of Judah" (Numbers 10:14). From almost the first mention of his name, the qualities demanded of a leader stand out in him. In the patriarchal and parting blessing upon his gathered sons Jacob likened him to a lion – the uncrowned king of the jungle – when he said, "Judah is a lion's whelp … who shall rouse him up? The sceptre shall not depart from Judah, till Shiloh come". Solomon's classification of the lion was one of four creatures "which went well and were comely in going". Number one was the lion, graded as "the strongest amongst beasts and turned not aside for any" (Prov.30:29–30).

Judah's penchant for storming the breach is brilliantly demonstrated in the part he played in placating Joseph and pleading for Benjamin, they being unaware that the austere Grand Vizier of Egypt was Joseph, their brother whom they had so shabbily misused. Joseph charged them with pilfering his divining cup. A search was made and the missing cup was found in Benjamin's sack. Stunned and incredulous, they all trooped back to Joseph's stately home. After being taken into Joseph's reception chamber, all standing a discreet distance from him, Joseph, Egypt's first lord, gave his verdict to keep Benjamin as his slave while allowing the others to return home to Jacob their venerable father. Of all verdicts this was the worst envisaged. More than mere words were required to change the inflexible decision of this all-powerful man. At this crucial juncture the king in Judah rose to the occasion, and took a bold step, a veritable death-or-glory action, for it reads, "Then Judah came near to him" and delivered the most pathetic and moving appeal recorded in the Bible. So stirring was it that it moved Joseph to end the charade and reveal his identity to his brothers, with words that stunned them, tersely saying, "I am Joseph". Their game was up: God had indeed found out their iniquity. They were all so terrified at his presence that Joseph had to invite his brothers to come near to him. Only then were they sufficiently composed to respond to his gracious, not imperious, invitation. They had thought him dead but were able to return back to their father with the greatest and most moving message he had ever heard, short and devoid of dressing: "Joseph is yet alive" (Gen.45:26).

Only one comparable, but far more vivifying message ever excelled it, which was the angel's, to the women, at the tomb of Joseph of Arimathæa, where they had last seen Jesus dead, who declared, "He is not here, He is risen" (Luke 24:6).

Joseph's divulging his true identity was a radical one indeed: he was not after all a haughty tyrant but Joseph their brother. Judah had broken the ice: their fears had been illusionary.

It was discreet counsel on the centurion's part to command all who could swim to leap into the water and make for the shore, and thereby allay the qualms of the others. Madame Curie's pioneering in the field of radium was costly. The cost was her own life and her daughter's, even before her own. But the benefits of her research with pitchblende have been incalculably enormous and beneficial.

* * * * * * * * * * * * * * * * * * * *

SERMON 26

ALL HOME AND SAFE

Acts 27:44: *And the rest, some on boards, and some on broken pieces of the ship. And so it came to pass, that they escaped all safe to land.*

For fourteen days and nights the travellers had suffered a period of anxiety and uncertainty, but with the arrival of day with the longed-for sight of land, hope was revived, which became reality when their feet felt the solid ground beneath them. Much more so when the promised salvation in Christ leaves the earnest seeker with a rock-firm – Christ is that Rock – foundation beneath him.

Paul had told them to bear up and cheer up, for there would be no casualties or loss of life. His confident assertion was given when there was no evidence of the storm's abatement. Sometimes God gives a promise of good or help in the teeth of conflicting evidence and this is always accompanied with the peace of God. Before the cause of the distress has been lifted every person's privilege is that of peace in the storm, in spite of the current turbulence. Christ powerfully stated this sentiment when rounding off His discourse, delivered in the Upper Room, which concluded His ministry. "These things have I spoken to you that ye might have peace. In the world ye shall have tribulation – trouble – but be of good cheer; I have overcome the world" (John 16:33).

When the census was taken of the ship's full complement the grand total of 276 was registered, which total tallied with the count taken when they were lined up on the beach, and is summed up in the revealing statement, "And it came to pass that they escaped all safe to land". How many times does the expression punctuate

198

the pages of the Bible when the odds have been against it? Israel's deliverance from Egypt was full and final. Their passage through the Red Sea was marred by no casualties: the host of pursuing Egyptians perished to a man, without a single survivor to report the calamity. On the contrary, Israel passed through the Red Sea as on dry land, while the Egyptians were drowned by the collapsing walls of water and their horses plunged and bucked in the quagmire and their chariots ground to a halt with slurried wheels (Exodus 14:14–29). There were no casualties of Israel's; there were no survivors of the Egyptians.

In the people's deliverance there is demonstrated an astonishing providence. Although the number who swam ashore is not given, it may be assumed that they would be relatively few. Even supposing that half of the ship's crew and company could swim, which is most unlikely, one is still left with the round figure of 140 who were in danger of drowning unless an alternative means of staying afloat could be provided, and this is what really happened. Already it had been noted that "the hinder part of the vessel had been broken by the violence of the waves". Significantly it does not say, 'was swept away', but was broken, by which operation God was providing a sufficient number of planks and fragments of wood to be used as life rafts and supports to keep the ones who could not swim afloat until the waves washed them onto the beach. A modern example of God's providence of a like kind is that of the evacuation of Dunkirk, where the beach was lined with tens of thousands of British soldiers – 300,000 in all, waiting to be taken off and brought back to England. All the time the Germans were advancing relentlessly, and threatened to take them prisoners or overwhelm them before enough shipping space could be found for them. In addition, the calmness of the sea furnished another feature of God's intervention by allowing the smallest craft to make the trip from the south-eastern harbours and ports of England, again and again, until the final contingent was rescued. At that particular time of the year the weather is notoriously stormy and unsettled. But the God "Who hath his way in the whirlwind and the storm", kept all such at bay, to facilitate the removal of a beleaguered army trapped between Hitler and the deep blue sea. No sooner had the operation been completed, than the weather pattern for that time of the year was resumed.

A further facet of God's providence displayed in the salvaging of 276 occupants of the ill-starred grain ship was the direction of the prevailing wind, which was in direct line with the creek or cove in which they hoped to thrust in the ship. Had it been a crosswind their hopes would have been dashed. A like providential control of the elements was experienced by the crew of the boat in which Columbus was set on discovering a western route to the Indies. His seamanship was all for tacking a north-westerly course, had not his men expostulated with him, crying "Follow the wind, Master! Follow the wind!" He listened to them and discovered the West Indies, and thereby missed finding North America by a hair's breadth. Had he continued on the course he had planned, North America would have fallen into the hands of Spain like a ripe plum and become a Catholic dominated country, which God had reserved for Protestant England.

Neither is the means of the travellers' safe arrival on Melita without some spiritual teaching. In the boards we discern a subtle reference to the cross of Christ from the planks of timber. Men with their aptitude for inventiveness and adaptiveness would, where possible, make use of rope lying around or cut lengths from the cordage to bind the boards together where broken off from the deck or body and stem of the ship. Two cross-pieces or sections of timber would form an improvised or crude raft, by which finally they were carried to safety.

That the cross of Christ is the stigma of the Gospel, none will deny. Paul stoutly maintained that the preaching of the cross or Christ crucified is the only means of salvation. Such preaching, however, is foolishness to the learned and philosophical Greeks, and a stumbling block to the religious and prejudiced Jews, but "to them which are called, both Jews and Greeks it is the power of God and the wisdom of God" (1 Cor.1:23–4). Paul also asserted that the preaching of the Cross is to those who are saved; that is saved now from their present sins and in the way of everlasting salvation, the power of God (1 Cor.1–18). John Wesley stated that the preaching of the Cross is "the greatest instrument of the power of God".

Augustus Toplady captured the truth of his salvation through "Christ and His cross alone", in the best known of his hymns, "Rock of Ages cleft for me, let me hide myself in Thee", a snatch of which runs: "Nothing in my hand I bring, Simply to Thy cross I cling". It would be no presumption to say that the dying thief received his enlightenment and inspiration of Christ's immediate ability and willingness to save him, from his focussed attention upon the inscription written over the cross: "THIS IS JESUS OF NAZARETH THE KING OF THE JEWS". Nor was it an accident or a frivolous gesture that the title was written in the three chief languages of the day, which served to stress the universality of the inscription, as only the combination of Hebrew and Greek and Latin could: Hebrew was the language of the religion, which eclipsed all others; Greek was the language of learning, which occasioned the aphorism "The Greeks had a word for it"; and Latin was the language of politics and militarism, which dominated the world of east and west. Christ's authority is supreme over these three areas, which make up the human lot.

His impassioned appeal is the expression of the breadth of his faith and of the scope of his understanding of Christ's identity and mission. If the superscription was true, the thief soundly reasoned that Jesus of Nazareth had a kingdom as kingdoms are the peculiar domain of kings. If Christ was a king then His prerogative was established. Obligation demands submission to the Supreme Pontiff. "LORD, remember me when Thou comest into Thy kingdom" was a prayer that grasped all these unique privileges, and as he was about to die and depart from this world, that he would outlive death and ascend to a heavenly kingdom. He understood that Christ was not a common felon, but God in a human form, offering life and immortality to all who believed and cast themselves upon Him unreservedly. That rough plank of the cross of Christ would save all who would do just that and, like the thief on His right side, cast themselves upon Him and lay hold of eternal life.

Of all those around the cross and among the sprawling crowd, including the disciples and the holy women, only one man was enlightened. The depth of his faith is staggering; he wouldn't let go. Christ's pronouncement when summing up one of His parables was never more applicable: "Many who are last shall be first and many who are first shall be last" (Matt.19:30). Of that company is the man who confessed Christ on a cross and got into the kingdom on a piece of timber or a plank, or a board.

Notice is also taken of those who got to land by making use of broken pieces of the ship. Life's voyage is full of broken things which have been redemptive to sinners in danger of losing their souls and forfeiting eternal life but tie up with Christ's sufferings and sacrifice. Disappointments which are the by-product of broken promises or broken marriages have been the means under God of salvaging many souls from an otherwise inescapable hell. A blind man when once testifying thanked God for his blindness, averring that "he never saw [Christ and heaven] until he became blind". A revelation of the meaning of the broken body of Christ has been a broken part of the ship which has carried many to heaven. Christ's moving words after He had broken the loaf of unleavened bread are among the most eloquent words ever spoken. "And supper being ended, He took bread, and when He had broken it, said, Take eat, this is My body which is broken for you, this do in remembrance of Me"(1 Cor.11:24). John Wesley records in his journal this amazing revelation about his mother. Although her life had been dedicated to God from early childhood and she brought up all her children in the fear of God so that none of her surviving children – thirteen in all – were lost eternally, she came to a full assurance of faith at eighty plus years of age, when partaking of the emblems at the communion rail: the broken bread and the cup, which fact is written upon her tombstone. And far from being unusual it has been the experience of numbers. Harriet Ward Beecher Stowe maintained that the inspiration to write the book *Uncle Tom's Cabin* was received and written immediately after a Holy Communion service. Further, it is claimed that the same book played a major part in the emancipation of the slaves in America.

Leigh Richmond was a godly minister of the Isle of Wight who is best known for his booklet titled *The Dairyman's Daughter*, which was the narration of an extraordinary young woman who died at nineteen years of age, and comprises the letters that she wrote to Richmond of her experiencing the spiritual blessings of the Gospel and of the intimate relationship she enjoyed with God. It has been translated into something like thirteen languages, and was much used in the conversion of sinners. A translation into Arabic produced a miniature revival in Turkey. He was travel-ling by stagecoach, from which he and his fellow passengers dismounted when approaching a steep incline, to lighten the load of the horses in their uphill pull. Leigh Richmond improved the occasion by distributing Christian booklets to those he met, one of whom showed his disdain and resentment by tearing the booklet in two before throwing it down, which provoked a fellow traveller upon observing the contemptuous gesture to remark to the godly minister, "That's one of your booklets wasted". "Don't be too sure about that" was the answer! Almost immediately a gust of wind blew the torn booklet over the hedge of a field, where farm labourers were working but had stopped for their midday break for lunch. One of them, on seeing the booklet sailing through the air and landing somewhere near, retrieved it and pieced it together, for the two parts were held together by a piece of cotton thread, which had not been broken. Some of the passengers couldn't help

LESSONS FROM THE VOYAGE OF LIFE

but notice the curious happening. The man who had recovered the booklet after putting the broken halves together began to read it out to the rest of the seated company. Leigh Richmond afterwards learned that all those men were converted and at least one became a minister of religion. A broken booklet filled with the Scripture was the means. Nor would it be any exaggeration to claim that a fairly voluminous book could be written of the large numbers who have been converted through broken instruments, as possibly the bulk of the 276 passengers onboard the Egyptian grain ship who made the safety of the shore on broken pieces of the ship.

And what shall we say more? Time would fail us to tell of broken bones and broken spirits and broken hearts, "A broken and a contrite heart O LORD Thou wilt not despise. The sacrifices of God are a broken spirit" (Psalm 51:17). A broken alabaster box of ointment received Christ's approval and earned one of the highest accolades that God ever honoured a human creature with. "She hath done what she could, this that she hath done shall be spoken of throughout the whole world" (John 12:7).

* * * * * * * * * * * * * * * * * * * *

SERMON 27

MELITA: A REVELATION OF CHRIST'S SALVATION

Acts 28:1–11: *And when they were escaped, then they knew the island was called Melita.*

Melita, consistent with the imagery of the allegory reveals the salvation that is in Christ. Only after their landing on the beach at Melita were they made aware of the identity of the island; and immediately afterwards the character of the people who lived there, or as in the wording of the text, "When they had escaped". It is a true saying that opines: "One has to live with a person to know them", and a parallel one is "That to know Christ one has to be in Him". Put in another way, "No one can know the Saviour without first being saved." To know a thing of a person and to know about them are vastly different things, and have little or nothing in common. John the apostle speaks of "Christ the Word of Life, which was from the beginning with the Father", as one whom "They the apostles had seen with their eyes and looked upon of the Word of Life" (1 John 1:1). He discriminated between "seeing with their eyes" and "which we have looked upon". The first implies a mere seeing or noticing, the second, "observing with careful attention", so as to take in the distinguishing features. Everyone in Christ is made aware of His singular virtues. Paul affirmed he had "no confidence in the flesh but rejoiced in Christ Jesus … counting all things but dung – and be found in Him … that I might know Him and power of His resurrection and the fellowship of his sufferings, being made conformable to His death" (Phil.3:9–10). To sum it up, Paul's supreme ambition was to aspire to an experiential knowledge of Christ, the antithesis of which is an intellectual one, and the possession of Christ as a complete Saviour, contrasting sharply with Christ as a partial deliverer, which consisted in nothing less than being raised from death in sin to all the life of love in Christ, conjoined with the risen life. In Christ was the satisfaction of being crucified with him, which connotes "death to the world and its attractions which the world loves, esteems and admires, such as its fashion, honour and its state" (John Wesley). Many who are versed with Christ's name are woefully ignorant of His person and purpose or His identity, and know nothing of His LORDSHIP and salvation. Their knowledge is that of a Christ after the flesh, or an historical Christ, but they are oblivious of His office as an exalted glorified Prince and Saviour. It is written, "He was in the world but the world knew Him not, He came unto His own, but His own received Him not, but as many as received Him to them gave He power to become the sons of God: which were born not of blood, nor of the will of the flesh nor of the will of man but of God" (John 1:10–13).

Unless a person reads the Bible and gives themselves wholly to it, they will never understand it and derive benefit from it. When, however, the reader applies himself to it, the Bible will reveal its treasures and its secrets. The writer recalls seeing a picture of the Taj Mahal at eight years of age and being impressed, but not until his late seventies did he see the actual building and was far more impressed.

One of the first things to impress the castaways was the spontaneous kindness of the island's inhabitants, which is a prime quality of God – the very first thing about Him – who has promoted the Gospel, which quality is emblazoned in a vignette of that Gospel spoken of in the epistle of *Titus*, where it is set off to the best advantage, as presented in a single paragraph that "not by deeds or righteousness that we have done, but after the kindness and love of God appeared … according to His mercy and washing of regeneration" (Titus 3:4–5). When describing the numerous qualities of love, the apostle places kindness before all the others, saying, "Love suffereth long and is kind" (1 Cor.13:4). Kindness belongs to the heart rather than the head and when attributed to God is further qualified as loving kindness. In Christ it is called compassion, and nowhere in the Bible is it more attractive than in the parable of the Good Samaritan, which has transmuted the word Samaritan into a household word, and has become synonymous with instant succour to the distressed, which it is impossible not to recognise. Ruth recognised it in Boaz, whose spontaneous comment was "Thou hast spoken friendly to me" (Ruth 2:13).

Where there are kind hearts there will be no harsh words, for speech is the very first vehicle of kindness: it never barks or bites. Luke calls the aborigines of Melita a barbarous people, meaning they were rude in speech and uncultured, quite unlike the polished Greeks and Romans, who had been groomed in the halls of learning and the academies of art. Melitians they were by birth and culture, but beneath their unannealed exteriors were gentle natures and much goodwill. Beneath the suavity and polish of the Roman culture the brute was only too ready to spring, as when they would have slain the prisoners, but the Melitians extended the warmth of kindness to them all.

Their brand of kindness is denominated "no ordinary kindness" which implies much more than the ordinary run-of-the-mill goodwill, and which was seldom to be seen in the more sophisticated circles, and far superior to the loudmouthed rudeness of Festus, to whom the cultured Paul returned a mild and soft answer.

Mark too, that the exemplary kindness was vouchsafed to strangers, with whom most people are reserved and suspicious. And because of the human tendency to abuse strangers, giving them short shrift, God commanded His Jewish people to "remember the stranger within the gates", while in the New Testament there is a strict command: "Be not forgetful to entertain strangers, for thereby some have entertained angels unawares" (Heb.13:2). One of the black spots that sully the book of Judges is the outrageous behaviour of the men of Benjamin towards the Levite's concubine (Judges 19:25– 8).

Melita thus prefigures that other island of mercy and goodness wherein dwells righteousness who bears the name Emmanuel, alias Christ the Saviour, in whom are no strangers. Once upon a time the residents of this world were "without Christ being aliens from the commonwealth of Israel and strangers from the covenants of promise – but now in Christ Jesus ye who sometimes were afar off are made nigh by the blood of Christ" (Ephes.2:12–13). "Now therefore, ye are no more strangers and foreigners, but fellow citizens with the saints and of the household of faith" (Ephes.2.19).

After fourteen days and nights of continuous rain it was still raining heavily, which, combined with the cold of the season, rendered the survivors soaked to the skin, which lent itself to great discomfort and mental distress. Such wretchedness soldiers had to endure in the trenches on the western front, while squelching in Flanders' mud. With such in mind, Paul's charge to Timothy to be strong in the grace in Christ Jesus that he might endure hardness as a good soldier of Jesus Christ, comes home with renewed force.

Many people come to Christ distressed and wretched – under the sense of the displeasure of God and soaked to their soul's depth by the small rain and great rain of His strength and impending judgement, and mourning their past delinquencies and wickedness. Among those whose minds have been filled with such distress may be numbered the prodigal and the woman who was a sinner; and all those with consciences "like troubled sea which cannot be quiet", with all those who come shivering and trembling feeling that their sins disqualify them from the love and mercy of God – not unlike the saloon keeper in America whose crooked roulette tables had ruined many of his patrons and had driven them to a suicidal grave, to mention not the least of his infamies. So troubled was he with a guilt-ridden conscience that he gave a recital of his wickedness to Finney in the very saloon where it had been committed. Putting his hand on his shoulder the Evangelist said, "Son, what a black story you've got to tell! But 'the blood of Jesus Christ God's Son cleanseth from all sin'" (1 John 1:7). From that moment the warmth in Christ began to dry the saloon keeper out and he smashed up the tables and poured out the liquor, until the floor was running with alcohol.

When prayer is at a premium and the young people remain unconverted while many people's lives are bound up with lasciviousness, liquor and lucre, be sure that the Son of Righteousness has departed to the winter solstice; spiritual coldness is in, and revival zeal is out.

In their kind action the people of Melita were demonstrating a love which is typical of Christ's love to buffeted and distressed sinners. The islanders' practical goodness epitomises the warmth of Christ's love, for it is credited to them that they kindled a fire to offset the discomfort and misery caused by the rain as well as the penetrating cold. Christ is characterised by the warmth of His love, concisely comprehended in Paul's bevy of 'ifs': "If there be any consolation in Christ, if any comfort of love, if any fellowship of the Spirit, if any bowels of mercy, fulfil ye my joy that ye be like-minded, having the same love" (Phil.2:1–2).

Coals of fire symbolise intense warmth of feeling and are depicted by Solomon in the Canticle where he likens their intensity and strength to the stance of death which once it lays hold of its victim never lets go, saying, "Its coals are coals of fire which hath a most vehement flame", literally meaning 'a coal of Jah', which is a shortened form of Jehovah (Song of Sol.6:6), and bespeaks an all-consuming love, such as "The zeal of My Father's house hath eaten Me up" (John 2:17).

In times of trouble and disaffection kindness is at a premium, but the troubles of the children of God are a spur to the goodness of God. When Paul wrote to the Corinthians he introduced God as "The Father of our LORD Jesus Christ, the Father of mercies and the God of all comfort, who comforteth us in all our tribulation, that we might be able to comfort them in any trouble with the comfort wherewith we are comforted of God" (2 Cor.1:3–4).

Christ is all zeal. True zeal is the expression of love and true love is heavenly fire, which is all-consuming. "Through idleness the house falleth through", but idleness gives place to energetic action when love supervenes and, far from falling into dilapidation, it is built up.

In spite of the pouring rain the kindly islanders kindled a fire, so that the shivering survivors would warm up and dry out, which is the immediate experience of all those who come to Christ. How quickly their former miseries are forgotten, like the woman in travail and therefore in sorrow alluded to by the LORD in John 16:21–2, "Who remembers no more her anguish for joy, as soon as she is delivered of a child". And so with sinners who come to Christ: their former coldness towards God is offset by a love and zeal for Christ.

Wet timber and, worse, still-damp tinder, does not bid fair for the lighting of a bonfire, and nothing less than a large blaze could serve the turn of almost 300 wet and bedraggled people, but the love of God makes short shrift of difficulties and frustrations. When General William Booth mooted his idea of a Salvation Army, a sceptic asked from where would he levy his officers to train his troops. Booth replied, "From the gutters" and so they came, from the alehouses, and the stews and the prisons.

As wet wood and damp combustibles are a damper upon endeavours to start a blaze, so unbelief is the greatest hindrance to promoting revival enthusiasm. As long as unbelief is in the saddle then zeal drags its feet. Many people amongst the children of God resent their complacency being disturbed, as was the case with the general populace at Jerusalem who were troubled with the arrival of the wise men enquiring, "Where is He that is born the King of the Jews?" (Matt.2:1–3) Of all people who might have been expected to encourage the builders of the walls of Jerusalem under Nehemiah's leadership were the men of Judah, yet they gave their voice against proceeding with such an impossible task.

They dampened the builders' ardour in saying, "The strength of the bearers of burdens is decayed, and there is much rubbish, so that we are not able to build the wall" (Neh.4:10). Before Lazarus could be brought out of the grave the ponderous rock-hard heart of unbelief had to be removed, Without such the dead in trespasses and sins will never revive and come forth into life and victory (John 11:29–34).

In the book *Lectures on Revival* written by Charles Finney, the author relates an incident which well illustrates the foregoing. A godly blacksmith felt the need of a move of God in the community. None of the young people were converted, the church prayer meetings were sparsely attended, the prayers were cold and formal, and a spirit of worldliness prevailed in the Fellowship, with the inevitable result that souls were not being saved. A great burden came upon him, so that he closed the smithy and gave himself to earnest prayer. Eventually he prevailed with God and became confident God would send revival. From the smithy he called upon the minister of his church and asked him to arrange a special meeting for prayer at the minister's residence. Neither the minister nor the members were impressed and objected that few would turn up. Notwithstanding, the minister deferred to the desire of the godly member and a Friday evening was set aside at the manse for specific prayer for revival. To everyone's surprise many came, and for a while there was no response, but the silence was broken by someone rising to their feet to ask for prayer for the salvation of their soul, to be quickly followed by another and yet another, and so it continued like a spiritual chain reaction. Upon their comparing notes later it transpired that everyone had come under deep conviction at the time the blacksmith had commenced praying in his forge, with the happy sequel of a gracious revival breaking out throughout the community. Indeed the blacksmith had shut down the forge-fire and had kindled a revival-fire that spread throughout the neighbourhood, and that, in spite of the coldness of discouragement and lack of enthusiasm. One of the gracious results of the awakening was that many of the young people in the community were converted.

Wherever the fire of zeal for God is kindled the comfort of Christ's love is enjoyed and the consolations of the Gospel counteract the discomfort – the wet clothes of irksome duties, and cold hearts. So conscious was Paul of the cold of a Roman prison that in his very last letter of invitation to Timothy he urged him to bring with him the cloak that he left at Troas with Carpus, and to come with all speed or, as he worded it, "Do thy diligence" (2 Tim.4:13,21). Far superior, nay infinitely so, to human comfort, is the love of God shed abroad in the heart by the Holy Ghost. Paul, in a similar vein, declared, "God who comforteth those who are cast down, comforted me by the coming of Titus" (2 Cor.7:6). Prior to the arrival of Titus with some of the brethren from Corinth, he had been "troubled on every side". There were fightings from the heathen without, and fears from false brethren within, and his soul had no rest, until comfort was brought with the cheering news of Titus and his companions (2 Cor.7:6).

Paul's humility was demonstrated in the part he played gathering sticks to fuel the fire, which provides the greatest impetus to revival: that of the ongoing salvation of souls saved and new converts brought to Christ.

In Christ Satan is helpless, which is highlighted in the epistle Paul wrote to the very Romans he was about to visit, saying, "Neither angels nor principalities nor powers shall separate us from the love of God which is in Christ Jesus" (Rom.8:38), a vivid illustration of which is found in this account. John wrote, "He that is born of God sinneth not, but he that is begotten of God keepeth himself, and that wicked one toucheth him not. And we know that we are of God and the whole world lieth in wickedness" (1 John 5:18–19). "And we are in Him that is true, even in His Son Jesus Christ" (1 John 5:20).

A critical moment ensued when a viper, stirred up by the heat of the fire, emerged from the burning faggots and fastened on Paul's

ROBERT COX

hand and hung on, having no intention to let go. Paul, however, had no intention to allow it the liberty, and shook off the venomous creature into the blaze while he carried on with his interrupted task. It would take more than a snake – however lethal – to deflect the apostle, however humble or high-flown. Evidently he readily concurred with the wise man's philosophy: "Whatsoever thy hand findeth to do, do it with thy might" (Eccles.9:10). One cannot help but observe that the fire that stirred up the serpent's enmity also destroyed it, like the revival that provokes persecution prevails over it by heaping coals of fire upon the heads of the persecutors.

To those in Christ the serpent becomes impotent for evil. John wrote: "He that is born of God sinneth not; but he that is begotten of God keepeth himself and that wicked one toucheth him not [that is to harm him] and we know we are of God, and the whole world lieth in wickedness" (1 John 5:18–19), "and we are in Him that is true, even in His Son Jesus Christ" (1 John 5:20).

Paul felt no harm after shaking off the vicious snake, which was so determined being stirred up by Satan that old serpent, who has yet to learn the futility of endeavouring to destroy those in Christ, as confirmed by this drama on the seashore. James crystallises this truth in his asseveration: "Let no man say when he is tempted, 'I am tempted of God': For God cannot be tempted with evil neither tempteth He any man, but every man is tempted when he is drawn away of his own lust and enticed [from his safe stronghold in Christ]" (James 1:13–14). Indeed, those in Christ are as safe as if they were in heaven.

To this present day it is reported that there are no poisonous snakes in Melita. One asserted of seeing a child eating a scorpion and suffering no harm. Of the barbarians it is written that they received them everyone, and their invitation was come and welcome. Later on in the story Luke relates that the chief man of the island, whose name was Publius, invited a representative section of the ship's company to his own home and received them and lodged them for three days with courtesy. Their action and

213

the entertainment extended to the survivors has its counterpart in Christ and is a gracious reminder of the welcome everyone receives who turn to Christ in their extremity. He extends a universal invitation to the flotsam and jetsam of this world – washed up on boards and broken pieces of the ship – in words as well-known as any He ever spoke, saying: "Come unto Me all ye that are weary and heavy laden, and I will give you rest. Take My yoke upon you, and learn of Me; for I am meek and lowly in heart: and ye shall find rest for your souls" (Matt.11:28–9).

Furthermore, in Christ the last Adam, all the problems that the first Adam brought upon himself and his posterity have been resolved and are typified in the dramatic episode of the father of Publius the chief man of the island, whose name equates to public. The father of Publius, who was prostrated with a dual affliction of fever and a bloody flux, is a typology of Adam the father and founder of the human race or the general public. Adam fell sick with the fever of sin, and as fever is synonymous with a high temperature, so Adam's sin constituted rebellion edged with an ambition for Godhead: "Ye shall be as gods", which was the tempting bait held out to Adam, at which he snatched (Gen.3:5), after it had appealed strongly to his ego and his pride. Moreover, fevers are highly infectious, so that the patients are confined to quarantine. Even so, the infection of sin is a far cry from the infection of fever, or, to change the figure, "Know ye not, a little leaven leaveneth the whole lump" (1 Cor.5:6). Sin's power of contagion has been well illustrated by the barrel of good apples in which is put an infected or rotten apple. In no time every apple in the barrel will have turned rotten. Paul stated the matter plainly, saying, "As by one man sin entered into the world, so death passed upon all men, for that all have sinned" (Rom.5:12). Combined with the fever, the father is said to have developed "a bloody flux" or a continuous haemorrhage, which meant that his life was ebbing away as his blood almost perceptively drained from him, to terminate prematurely the life of the sufferer: as the Bible reminds us,

"The life of the flesh is in the blood" (Lev.17:11).

Adam, the father of the people or the federal head of the human family, has been granted a stay of execution through Christ the Last Adam, and typified in Paul through Christ. Paul elsewhere is said to be found in Christ, ministering the glorious power of His resurrection and able to say, "I am crucified with Christ, nevertheless, I live, yet not I, but Christ liveth in me … I live by the faith of the Son of God, who loved me and gave himself for me" (Gal.2:20). Through the ministry of the apostle laying his hands on the father of Publius, signifying his transferring divine life, the law of the Spirit of life in Christ Jesus set him free from the law of sin – the fever and death – the bloody flux. And it is profitable to observe that the hand which had shaken off the viper into the fire was the hand that was laid upon the father of Publius and brought him life and deliverance; only prayerful and holy hands or hearts can instil heavenly life and salvation. James wrote, "Draw near to God and He will draw near to you: resist the devil and he will flee from you" (James 4:77–8). Moses' hands carried the Law of God's holiness (Exodus 34:29). Those same hands held the rod of God's power and authority (Numbers 20:11).

* *

ACTS 27

[1] AND when it was determined that we should **sail into Italy**, they delivered Paul and certain other prisoners *un*to *one* named Julius, a centurion of Augustus' band. [2] And entering into a ship of Adramyttium, we launched, meaning to sail by the coasts of Asia; *one* Aristarchus, a Macedonian of Thessalonica, being with us. [3] And the next *day* we touched at Sidon. And Julius courteously entreated Paul, *and* gave *him* liberty to go unto *his* friends to refresh himself. [4] And when we had launched from thence, we sailed under Cyprus, because the winds were contrary.

[5] And when we had sailed over the sea of Cilicia and Pamphylia, we came to Myra, *a city* of Lycia.

[6] And there the centurion found a ship of Alexandria sailing into Italy; and he put us therein. [7] And when we had sailed slowly many days, and scarce were come over against Cnidus, the wind not suffering us, we sailed under Crete, over against Salmone; [8] And, hardly passing it, came unto a place which is called The Fair Havens; nigh whereunto was the city *of* Lasea.

[9] Now when much time was spent, and when sailing was now dangerous, because the Fast was now already past, Paul admonished *them*, [10] And said unto them, "Sirs, I perceive that this voyage will be with hurt and much damage, not only of the lading and ship, but also of our lives."

[11] Nevertheless the centurion believed the master and the owner of the ship, more than those things which were spoken by Paul. [12] And because the haven was not commodious to winter in, the more part advised to depart thence also, if by any means they might attain to Phenice, *and there* to winter; *which is* an haven of Crete, and lieth toward the south west and north west.

[13] And when the south wind blew softly, supposing that they had obtained *their* purpose, loosing *thence*, they sailed close by Crete.

[14] But not long after there arose against it a tempestuous wind, called Euroclydon.

[15] And when the ship was caught, and could not bear up into the wind, we let *her* drive. [16] And running under a certain island which is called Clauda, we had much work to come by the boat: [17] Which when they had taken up, they used helps, undergirding the ship; and, fearing lest they should fall into the quicksands, strake sail, and so were driven.

[18] And we being exceedingly tossed with a tempest, the next *day* they lightened the ship; [19] And the third *day* we cast out with our own hands the tackling of the ship. [20] And when neither sun nor stars in many days appeared, and no small tempest lay on *us*, all hope that we should be saved was then taken away.

[21] But after long abstinence Paul stood forth in *the* midst of them, and said, "Sirs, ye should have hearkened unto me, and not have loosed from Crete, and to have gained this harm and loss. [22] And now I exhort you to be of good cheer: for there shall be no loss of *any man's* life among you, but of the ship. [23] For there stood by me this night *the* angel of God, whose I am, and whom I serve, [24] Saying, "Fear not, Paul; thou must be brought before Caesar: and, lo, God hath given thee all them that sail with thee."

[25] "Wherefore, sirs, be of good cheer: for I believe God, that it shall be even as it was told me. [26] Howbeit we must be cast upon a certain island."

[27] But when *the* fourteenth night was come, as we were driven up and down in Adria, about midnight the shipmen deemed *that* they drew near to some country; [28] And sounded, and found *it* twenty fathoms: and when they had gone a little further, they sounded again, and found *it* fifteen fathoms. [29] Then fearing lest we should have fallen upon rocks, they cast four anchors out of the stern, and wished for *the* day.

[30] And as the shipmen were about to flee out of the ship, when they had let down the boat into the sea, under colour as though they would have cast anchors out of *the* foreship, [31] Paul said to

the centurion and to the soldiers, "Except these abide in the ship, ye cannot be saved."

[32] Then the soldiers cut off the ropes of the boat, and let her fall off.

[33] And while *the* day was coming on, Paul besought *them* all to take meat, saying, "This day is *the* fourteenth day *that* ye have tarried and continued fasting, having taken nothing. [34] Wherefore I pray you to take *some* meat: for this is for your health: for there shall not an hair fall from the head of any of you." [35] And when he had thus spoken, he took bread, and gave thanks to God in presence of *them* all: and when he had broken *it*, he began to eat. [36] Then were *they* all of good cheer, and they also took *some* meat.

[37] And we were *in* all in the ship two hundred threescore and sixteen souls.

[38] And when they had eaten enough, they lightened the ship, and cast out the wheat into the sea.

[39] And when it was day, they knew not the land: but they discovered a certain creek with a shore, into the which they were minded, if it were possible, to thrust in the ship. [40] And when they had taken up the anchors, they committed *themselves* unto the sea, and loosed the rudder bands, and hoisted up the mainsail to the wind, and made toward shore. [41] And falling into a place where two seas met, they ran *the* **ship aground;** and the forepart stuck fast, *and* remained unmoveable, but the hinder part was broken with the violence of the waves. [42] And the soldiers' counsel was to kill the prisoners, lest any *of them* should swim out, *and* escape. [43] But the centurion, willing to save Paul, kept them from *their* purpose; and commanded that they which could swim should cast *themselves* first *into the sea, and* get to land:

[44] And the rest, some on boards, and some on *broken pieces* of the ship. And so it came to pass, that they escaped all safe to land.

* * * * * * * * * * * * * * * * * * * *